Starmaker Machinery

MEREDITH M DAY

Copyright © 2017, 2008 by Meredith M Day

All rights reserved. No part of this book may be reproduced in any form or by any electronic or mechanical means, including information storage and retrieval systems, without permission in writing from the publisher, except by reviews, who may quote brief passages in a review.

ISBN: 978-1-929893-05-8 (Paperback edition)

ISBN 978-1-532357-11-4 (eBook edition)

SUMMARY: Expert insider guide for Actor and Musician self-promotion. Includes top-secret "End Runs" and short cuts for self-promotion not available to the public. Written by Celebrity Talent Management and Development Expert Meredith M. Day

DISCLAIMER: As Einstein says, "I am a mathematician, not an arithmetician." I appreciate knowing about any typos you may find reading this book! *Meredith Day*

Distributed by Bublish Inc.

Printed and bound in the USA First Printing June 2018

Published by RodJRay

DEDICATION

In honor of all the talented young performers I have had
the privilege of helping to fulfill their dreams..

	Acknowledgments	i
1	Do You Have The Gift?	1
2	The Actor That has "It"	5
3	When To Start Your Acting Career	9
4	Improvisation And The Audition	18
5	The Actor's Clothes And Hair	23
6	The Actor's Pictures	26
7	The Actor's Resume	32
8	The Actor's Reel	35
9	Finding An Agent	38
10	Is My Agent Or Manager Is Any Good?	44
11	Do I Need A Manager?	49
12	When To Hire Publicist	53
13	School For The Young Working Actor	56
14	The Casting Agent Relationship	59
15	The Audition	63
16	The Call Back	69
17	The Cold Read Audition	72
18	Joey Paul On The Cold Read	76
19	The Ice Cold Read	79
20	From The Producers Perspective	81
21	What Does An Acting Career Cost?	84
22	Managing Your Child Actor's Money	87
23	Maintaining Family Sanity	91
24	On Set Behavior	95
25	The Actor's Survival Kit	100

26	Networking On And Off Set	102
27	Recommended Publications For Actors	105
28	Heasdheets and Resumes	107
29	Audition Records	109
30	I've Got A Series, Now What Do I Do!	111
31	The Music Business	113
32	About Band Management	117
33	Building a Fan Base	119
34	Live Gig Dos And Don'ts	124
35	Live Show Guidelines	129
36	Recording Studio Guidelines	140
37	Lyric Writing Guidelines	146
38	Pumping The Gig	150
39	Seeking Band Investment	157
40	How To Manage Promotion	160
41	Social Media Promotion	163
42	How Often Should My Band Play?	166
43	Idols and Voices – Life Changing	169
44	Go Do It!!!	174
45	How To Avoid Sexual Harassment	176
46	Suggested Reading	181
	About The Author	185

ACKNOWLEDGMENTS

To Ethlie Ann Vare for teaching me how to write coherently.

To Mary E Case for teaching me "You can do anything you put your mind to."

DO YOU HAVE THE GIFT?

Welcome to a true operations manual for the aspiring actor and musician. You are receiving all the secrets I have learned over the years marketing theatrical and musical talent.

Nothing worthwhile is easy. If you are willing to learn and work your behind off you will succeed. The most important thing to remember is:

THE RULES ARE:

THERE ARE NO RULES!

MEREDITH M DAY

THE BAD NEWS

Perhaps you are surrounded by adoring people telling you how cute and talented you or your child is. Telling you that you should get an agent. You're thinking about it. Several have told you about agents to call.

Then one day you get a call from an "agent". They tell you that you have been selected for an "audition".

Perhaps you have seen an ad in the newspaper, "Audition: Actors needed, all types".

In the back of your mind a small voice tells you it's a scam (99.9999% chance it is), but you know you are talented, and you agree to go to the audition despite your qualms.

When you arrive, you are horrified to see there are dozens of "actors" present. The audition is a "Cattle call".

After the "audition" you are told that you have "great potential". You are told that if you will take classes and have pictures shot, there is no doubt that you will get bookings.

The cost for the classes and pictures seems to range from $1500 to $6000 dollars. A sliding scale directly proportional to your willingness and capability to pay.

Strictly speaking, the company is right on target. In order to get work an actor MUST take regular coaching classes and have pictures taken. But these companies are in business PRIMARILY to sell poor unsuspecting actors as much as they can in the way of classes and pictures.

This is their main business, not getting the talent work.

These companies have no intention of limiting selection to actors that are truly gifted. They will take pretty much anyone who will come to an "audition".

They will then fleece the actor for as much money as they can. When the money runs out so does their interest. They "file and forget" the actor.

THE EXCEPTION

For the aspiring actor, companies such as John Robert Powers has become very aggressive in bringing in scouts from industry to do workshops and scout for talent.

Though John Robert Powers is known to take all comers, they provide an extremely valuable beginners training ground with their "On camera" workshops and other coaching classes. These are available at some of their locations.

For years known as primarily a modeling school, Powers and others like them have expanded the scope to provide very high quality TV, film and commercial training for the beginning aspiring actor.

These workshops are crucial, as an actor cannot attract better coaches, high-level agents or managers without preliminary training.

MEREDITH M DAY

THE ACTOR THAT HAS "IT"

The performer who can succeed in the entertainment industry is the one who stands in the middle of the floor at family gatherings and entertains the guests out of sheer energetic joy.

He is the performer who can't resist talking to strangers in the checkout line. He is the first performer in line to enter the school talent show. He is the performer who, since he was able to talk, has told EVERYONE that he wants to be "AN ACTOR!" or "A MUSICIAN!" OR "A STAR!".

The successful performer is not afraid of looking stupid, will do anything for a laugh. Does not freak out when lost, he views it as an adventure. He is able to look anyone right in the eye and carry on a conversation. Most importantly, he is willing and able to follow detailed directions FROM STRANGERS.

Performers that have "The Gift" are many times considered a pain by those around them. They always want to be in the middle of the action. On the "X" when the light turns on.

If you need to decide if the entertainment business is right for you or your child, picture that you will have to walk into a room filled with strangers, and deliver cheerfully with style and verve.

Parents or friends are NOT allowed into the audition. If you are cautious or frightened in new situations, you will not prosper in this environment. You will find it unpleasant and upsetting.

The truly successful performer LIVES for those moments he is allowed to be in the spotlight. All the rest of his life is just waiting for those magic "spotlight" moments.

As Blake Lively's father, acting coach Ernie Lively, says, "We are not actors, we are "auditioners", if we are really good at auditioning, very occasionally we get to be actors." Can you handle that?

Can you handle one job for every 30 or 40 auditions? Can you handle three jobs out of 200 auditions? Can you handle the rigors of going time and time again to those auditions?

STARMAKER MACHINERY

You can, if it's your life dream, your ultimate goal! Then you will handle it!

An actress who I discovered, developed and managed, Margo Harshman ("Tawney Dean" on "Even Stevens" now a regular, "Delilah", on NCIS), had 100 auditions her second year. She auditioned 200 times before getting her first "big" role.

Her wonderful mother, Janelle, drove her 120,000 miles from Carlsbad California to Hollywood, to and from auditions in 2 years. Deducting the weekends, that meant that she averaged more than one audition every 2.5 days of the 2nd year. Could your family confront that?

Margo's family made the sacrifice of moving to be closer to the auditions. The Grandmother had to move in with them to help care for the rest of the kids as the mother was on the road so much with Margo. They even put a "port o potty" in the van for Margo.

The only reason the family was willing to put up with it was that Margo had known from the day she was born she wanted to be "AN ACTRESS". She was dragging the mother, not visa versa.

Today Margo is a very successful character actress with multiple TV series and leading roles in films to her credit. She works all the time.

It's the same as when a kid is out in the driveway shooting baskets till 3 in the morning because he loves to do it. That kid truly wants to be a basketball player, and the parent

SHOULD pony up for a private coach. The best they can find in their local area. Or move the family to be close to a great coach!

By the same token, if you are a class clown, a show off, are intimidated by strangers and live to be center stage, then yes. Green light. Go find the very best training you can. In this case it's a good investment.

If you would rather be playing soccer, or doing the "mall", if you're a shy homebody, forget it. No matter what your friends or parents tell you to do.

The challenge is to find what you are passionate about and nurture it. Just because your friends think you are cute is no reason to push yourself into something you aren't passionate about doing.

WHEN TO START YOUR ACTING CAREER

WHAT JOEY PAUL SAYS ABOUT THE ACTOR

According to Award Winning Casting Director Joey Paul, an actor needs to be "WELL TRAINED".

There will be many actors with much longer resumes, and the jobs will go to those actors. It's very hard for an older actor to get a break. The older aspiring actor must be very well trained.

Ms. Paul states that it is very difficult to enter the business as a teenager or young adult. "You need to be drop dead gorgeous, very talented and/or extraordinarily unique to get a part as a teen or young adult newcomer."

Customarily all the teen and young adult parts go to "old timers", actors who started when they were very young children and are extremely well seasoned

It doesn't seem fair that it is so hard to break into the industry if you don't have the experience. You have to understand that there are literally thousands of dollars being spent per minute on the set, and an untrained or unruly actor can cost the producer a fortune, or worse, cost him his job.

The bottom line is - Training, Training, Training, and Workshop, Workshop, Workshop. Becoming an actor is the same as becoming a lawyer, only more demanding, and there is no middle class. It took Harrison Ford twenty years of supporting himself with set construction to become an "overnight success".

If you don't pay the dues, going to workshop religiously every week and doing any and all free jobs you can snag to build your resume, you will not float to the top.

GO FOR THE GOLD

Think of it this way, if you want to be a track star you have to run every day, if you want to be an actor you have to act. The average actor will never have enough jobs or auditions to stay polished. There is little feast; mostly there is famine. During the slow times it is imperative that the skills be kept fluid with workshop.

As we will discuss later, stage is the exact OPPOSITE of

film, television and commercials.

If the actor has extensive stage background, this very often is viewed as a NEGATIVE on the film and television resume. If you play soccer, you don't train for baseball. If you want to be a film or television actor, DON'T train for stage. Stage requires very big acting; film and television require great subtlety.

It is possible to be successful in both realms, but the training is completely opposite. Think of stage as football, and television and film as figure skating. They are completely different worlds.

WHAT TO DO FIRST

The common misconception is that the first move is to get an agent. Then the agent will get your actor a bunch of auditions, and a bunch of work. This is absolutely WRONG. Here is the proper schedule of events:

1. Acting Coach/Workshop

2. Pictures

3. Manager

4. Agent

5. Publicist

The exception is the infant. Obviously, training is not an issue, but socialization is. If you are frightened in a crowd of strange people, don't become an actor. If you are a fussy, cranky person, don't become an actor. You'll hate it

If you exhibit the "free spirit" described in the last chapter, then first you must get the proper training. Think of it like ice-skating or track. If the actor is not properly trained he will fall flat on his face and embarrass everyone. An agent will certainly not sign him, unless he is extraordinarily gifted. This is not usually the case. Usually he's just a nice guy (girl) who wants to be an actor.

FINDING A COACH

When you decide that an acting career is the direction you want to go, the first and most important move is the acting coach.

Unfortunately, the perception is to be an actor you first must have and agent. This is wrong. The actor must first be trained. THEN seek out an agent.

The most affordable training is in high school and Jr. College. Most now have great TV and Film departments.

The best way to find a good acting coach is to check with several reputable talent agents in your area. Call and ask if they can recommend a workshop for your age actor. Make sure it is an agent that represents your age. Be sure to tell the agent that you will call for an audition for when the coach says you are ready. They will be amazed at how savvy you are. They may even remember you.

When you call don't insist on speaking to the agent directly. If they are not available the receptionist is fully capable of giving you the information you need. Be appreciative, courteous. The entertainment industry is a very small town. There is nothing more entertaining than discussing "psycho wanna bees". Word gets around fast.

You must look around your community and find the best coach you can to train you in the art of auditioning. No matter how good an actor you are, if you don't have auditioning skills you will never get a chance to act.

YOUR COACH

THEATRICAL V.S. FILM

A common misconception is that theatrical training prepares an actor for film. IT DOES NOT!

Live stage coaching is a detriment. You must understand that in theatre an actor must project sound and expression to the back of the theater. He must be big, loud, very exaggerated.

In film the camera is as close as six inches away. It is the opposite; everything must be understated, subtle. Low key. If you move six inches you could disappear from the picture. You can accomplish with a 1/4" move of the eyebrow what it takes great-exaggerated body movement to convey in the live theater onstage.

Many actors who are successful in the Theatre wish to move into film. They need to re train themselves just as an athlete who plays football must completely re train to figure skate.

Unfortunately, sadly, many actors think that because they are the darlings of their local Theatre Company they will be the darlings of film. Not unless they retrain themselves. They have to "woodshed".

Most theatrically trained actors hit a brick wall when they get feedback from their first film auditions. "Way too big, sorry."

The first step is to find a Drama school or community theatre group that that offers "on camera" acting classes. Start here prior to looking for a professional coach. These classes will bring you up to the level of skill that is acceptable to a professional coach.

At the second level, when you have your basic on camera training you now will need to move up to a professional acting (on camera) coach.

In looking for a professional film acting coach you will want to find one who is coaching WORKING actors. Do not go to a modeling school, unless the actor wants to be a model.

If a school touts themselves as strong in film, ask them for a list of WORKING actors they have trained. Call that actor's agent and ask for a reference on the school. Anyone can say they trained someone; you need to verify the credits.

STARMAKER MACHINERY

The most reliable way to be referred to a good acting coach is to call a reputable talent agent in your area (get a list from the Screen Actor's Guild in Los Angeles or New York) and ask for the name of a few coaches they respect. Tell them that you are interested in acting and you would like to go to a good coach prior to seeking an agent. This will give them a real buzz. Rarely are "newbie" actors that smart.

Until you have been with a coach for a few months DO NOT ask for an audition with a talent agent. When you are good enough, the coach will tell you, and they help you get an audition with an agent or two. You will come in the door with the recommendation of a person the agent respects. And, more importantly, you will be well trained, ready to enter the fray. You will be a "contendah". You will be very powerful.

When you are ready to present yourself to agents, your coach will be happy to help. Your success get the coach more work, so the coach is very motivated to help promote their talented well trained actors. It gets them more work!

A reputable acting coach will charge from $150 to $250 per month for acting workshop. This is a must for all serious actors.

Private coaching sessions cost in the range of $75 to $200 per session. Private coaching is done by the actor's coach, prior to an audition. Generally the workshop classes are one night per week. NEVER pay for more than one month at a time.

Watch other actors in your coaching classes, you will learn as much as they do. You will also be able to compare you proficiency level against the over all class, you will know if you can make it yet or if you need more time.

If you are not having fun and not cutting it, then back to the soccer. If you are really passionate, but feel you are not getting up to speed, you may want to change your coach. Maybe their technique is not "gellin" with you.

If you want to act in film, you also have to decide if you're willing to uproot your family. (If you have one) If you don't live in an area where there is work in film you will have to move to the appropriate area. That would be Los Angeles, New York, Orlando, Montreal or Vancouver. The majority of all film work is there in North America, in that order.

WORST DOWNSIDE SCENARIO

When you find a good coach, you should train for a minimum of three months of weekly workshops prior to seeking an agent. That is the very minimum time required to get you up to speed and competitive. Even after you get an agent you will want to work out weekly with your acting coach for the same reason, track stars work out to be in top form.

Even for the very successful actor, jobs are far and few. If you don't work out you will loose the skills.

STARMAKER MACHINERY

If your agent has a coach they really respect, try them. Every different coach you work with will bring you new perspective and skill.

TVI Actor's studio in Los Angeles and New York are great because they bring in many different coaches for the actor to work with as well as providing many other necessary services such as free casting director mailing labels.

To put it into perspective, an actress I worked with made $12,000 in the first quarter of a year. But the money was based primarily on work she had done in the last year. The first quarter of the next year she has had only one job.

To put it into perspective, an actress I worked with made $12,000 in the first quarter of a year. But the money was based primarily on work she had done in the last year. The first quarter of the next year she has had only one job.

But meanwhile she goes religiously to workshop every week. When she is called for an audition she is a well-oiled machine.

IMPROVISATION AND THE AUDITION

One of the most valuable aspects of weekly workshop is the development of a war chest of characters.

Many times on an audition an actor is not given any direction. Based on the script in hand, the actor will be able to bring forward one of the characters he uses in his weekly improvisation class. It is no crime to steal a character from a workshop mate if you need to.

It is also important to study everyone you meet. You may be able to use their character at some point!

Workshop classes are especially important for actors who have never had any "hard knocks". What makes a great actor is a reservoir of emotion to draw on, both good and bad.

If you have had a very pleasant upbringing, have never been without, then you will probably not be able to bring forward that deep emotion on demand. A good coach will help you find and identify that emotion so when it's needed it's there for you.

If you are a passionate actor, watch as many movies as you can. That's is a valuable place to learn how to act. Study the great, Academy Award winning actors. Study actors you would like to be like.

Study crazy, loopy actors, you may need them someday. Watch a video over and over if it's a good one. You will learn from the actors on screen. Imitate the acting and dialogue. You will be able to pull up Jim Carey or Rod Steiger, or Melissa McCarthy when you need that type of character.

Use great actors onscreen as your coaches too! Imitate their great lines.

If you are an actor, be an actor, don't repress it. Don't be quiet in the checkout line. If you want to interact, go for it.

If you're an aspiring comedian, be one. Use the checkout line as your rehearsal room. If you get a laugh you're material is working. If people are mad at you, it's not. If your joke doesn't work yet, keep working on it. Be honest. with yourself. If something isn't quite dialled in, keep working on it. Dial it in.

THE MAGICAL REFERRAL

Years ago I was an actor. I did plays at the Pasadena Playhouse. I was the token 'kid" for the Playhouse college student productions.

A director liked me, thought I had talent. He suggested to my parents that they enroll me in a workshop. Way back then my parents didn't understand that was a very valid referral from an industry professional.

My parents only saw the price tag.. $14 dollars per week (a long time ago!)! My parents passed on the workshop. They didn't understand that the reason that I had been referred to workshop was that the director thought I had talent. He wanted to see what I could do. They passed, and I missed a wonderful opportunity.

A few years later the Universal Studios New Talent Department auditioned me. Again they recommended a workshop across the street from Universal Studios. The price tag was $80 for four weeks. Again, stupidly, I passed because of the price tag. Had I known what I know now, I would have come up with the money!

What I still didn't know then was that the reason they wanted me to take the workshop was so that they could see if I could act! Get the coaches assessment of my capabilities. Maybe also they liked my look but I did a crummy audition, and they were trying to help me. In any case I passed on a wonderful opportunity.

STARMAKER MACHINERY

When you find a reputable coach the price tag will seem to be expensive. Worst downside: You take the workshop and do not develop enough to compete in the film business. Or perhaps you find you prefer to be on the football field. At the very least you will develop skills you can use in whatever you do later!

No matter what, you will come out of that workshop with much more confidence than you went in. The workshop will benefit you in public speaking skills such as student politics and verbal reports. It is definitely a worthwhile crap shoot. The skills you will learn will benefit you for the rest of your life. It will give you great power.

Best upside, you will excel and the coach will take you in hand and be sure you get a good agent and maybe even a manager. Think of it this way, coaches love to flaunt their successes, it gets them more work.

THE WEEKLY WORKOUT

As we have discussed, successful actors workout regularly to keep their skills honed. Jobs are far between, and the actor must be very well trained and a highly greased acting machine for all the auditions required to get those prized bookings.

At first the coach will focus on building the basic skills of the new student. Secondly the coach will work on refinements and building a retinue of improvisational characters you will bring forward on auditions as needed.

This retinue, stable of characters, is imperative for a highly skilled actor. On an audition there is no time to think about what you are going to do, it has to come instantly and with panache. If you are skilled at improvisation, and can "turn on a dime" from one character to another, you will be a success.

Just as a member of a band needs to know the songs well enough to do them without thinking, the actor needs to know his variety of characters to be able to do them without thinking.

Jobs are based on two things: Talent and Resume. A good coach will dial in the talent. The resume will be built by the actor, coach referrals, the manager and the eventual agent.

THE ACTOR'S CLOTHES AND HAIR

CLOTHES

There is a very common misconception among aspiring actors that you must be dressed up for auditions. That is far from the truth. Generally the director or casting associate is looking for "real people".

They don't want little girls that look like Jon Benet Ramsey, unless that is the part. They don't want Baywatch types. They want real, the girl or guy next door. From that perspective don't slick the hair down. Don't send the clothes to the dry cleaner.

Wear what you feel the character you are reading would wear. Don't "Dress to impress" unless that is the character.

You should be clean, well groomed, if your jeans have a rip in the knees, no big deal. The default outfit for young adult actors is jeans a casual shirt with perhaps a sweater thrown over the shoulders. Clean fingernails!

If the sides (script) indicates a certain look, then come as close as you can out of your actor's wardrobe. Don't go buy something for every audition, you'll go broke. Surfing the thrift store is a great way to build up wardrobe. The clothes should look lived in anyway.

HAIR

If you have an extreme hair cut you will limit your parts. A middle of the road cut that can be styled a few different ways is good.

For the female, the hair should not be too long or too short. Bangs are good. A style with no bangs tends to look severe if they want the hair pulled back. The forehead is very reflective on camera, it takes away from the eyes. You can always spray the bangs back if they do want a severe look.

If you have very long hair you may miss a part. There's not much you can do with really long hair, and the director hates to cast someone who objects to cutting their hair. If your hair is very long, they will assume it would be unpleasant for you to be asked to cut it, and they will pass on you for an actress that has a more appropriate hair style.

Young boys should have hair long enough to flop around or be brushed back to one side. Don't have it so long it obscures his face without hair spray. This will knock him out of the running in most cases. Always be willing to cut hair for a part.

Study TV shows and movies, commercials as well. Notice the length of the actor's hair in your category. Notice the hair styles.

Be consistent with you hair. Keep it looking the length of your headshot. It's ok to vary the "do" but make sure that what is on your head sheet is what walks in the door length wise.

PUTTING YOUR BEST FACE FORWARD

Your picture is your calling card. It's what sells you before you're in the door, and what will certainly clinch the deal after the audition. Your headshot must truly represent you in look AND personality.

Theatrical and commercial photography is an art, you can't get it at the mall. Your coach or agent will recommend someone that they know does a good job. Someone who shoots the kind of pictures that are successful with casting agents.

Before hiring the photographer, look at their portfolio. If you don't like the pictures keep looking, move on. The good photographers are not cheap. See who they have in their portfolio. Are they recognizable working actors?

STARMAKER MACHINERY

You will need a variety of shots to choose from. Dress in casual clothing. Dress to your type. Bring a lot of clothes to choose from. The photographer will know what will look good in the picture. What will compliment your look and body type. If you are a perfect banker type wear a suit.

Always include a casual shot in your photo session. A nice worn denim jacket over a casual shirt is always a good choice. Your agent or manager will know better than you what look is your most "saleable'. Make sure to provide a good shot of that look to your agent or manager.

Don't dress in white or light pastels. Dressing in really light colors detract from your face. The light color becomes the focal point.

Avoid very dark clothing as well. Denim photographs great as do patterns such as plaid. White deters from you face as it becomes the brightest spot in the picture.

As mentioned earlier, a good coach will know of a photographer that is good with actors and knows the necessary "look" that will "book".

If you are not feeling well on picture day, cancel the shoot! RESCHEDULE!!!! You will be wasting your money if you take pictures when you are not feeling well. The energy will be lacking, you will look "off". You will not book from the shots.

Before you have any prints made, or put anything online, let your coach or agent look at the proofs. Do not choose the pictures yourself. Absolutely DO NOT let your spouse or parents have a vote! Have your pictures chosen by an industry professional.

It's very difficult to judge your own pictures. You will focus on what you don't like which might be the very feature that will imprint you on others, creating you as a unique talent.

What your friends and relatives may like may be just too "sweet" for a head shot. Pictures that put Grannie "in a wad" generally are not the right ones for your acting career. Your coach will know what look the agent and casting agents want. Trust them.

THE PICTURES

TVI in New York City and Van Nuys, California have many industry photographer's work on display in their facility. Their displays include contact information. You will need a "commercial" and a "theatrical" shot. TVI has many excellent entertainment photographers on display in the foyer that do all ages.

The commercial shot is very high energy, a nice animated, accessible smile. For theatrical you will need both smile and serious (sexy) shots. Ask your coach to show you what kind of headshot is currently in fashion. The trends change, and you want your actor's promotional material to look current.

STARMAKER MACHINERY

If you or your child has an agent they will want the look of the headshot to be consistent with the look of their roster. They will recommend a photographer that will give them the look. They will want their logo on the headshot and recommend a duplicator that will set the shots up properly on the sheet. Take an example of your agent's other headshots for the duplicator or digital artist to go by.

The agent may do all their casting submitting online. In this case they will give you the specs of the digital file they need and exactly how they want it set up.

You will order one 8x10 glossy or 300 dpi digital file of each picture you want to use from the photographer for paper prints. Each "master" 8x10 print will cost from 20 to 35 dollars.

The digital files are usually a little less. Those you generally get from the photographer. If your agent wants paper duplicates they will tell you where to take them for duplication.

You NEVER give away the master shot or digital file. Ever! Nowadays, most casting is done online, so the digital files are the most important.

Nowadays with everything digital, it is common for the photographer also to do any retouching needed. They will delete a funny hair or facial blemish. Very important; be cautious not to have the photographer retouch the photo to such and extent that it does not look like you in person. That will cost you parts!

Prior to being signed by an agent, the head sheet should carry the name of the actor and leave room for an agent's sticker. Until you have an agent you can use a sticker with your contact number and email or link on it.

Don't print a zillion head sheets. When you get an agent you will need to reprint the head sheets with their logo and contact information on it if they tell you too. Again, most casting is done nowadays online, so the agent may just need to have your digital file. They may ask you to sign up for a site like ActorsAccess.com.

It is very cost effective in the beginning to set the head sheet up in a file that can be printed in low quantities at a place like FedXOffice if needed. They have great thick, glossy paper which looks great in the beginning. Just print a few at a time.

With child actors it is not good to spend a fortune on pictures as they grow so quickly they will need to update often.

You also must update any time there is a different hair cut or significant weight change. Many times a call comes because of a "look". If you do not look like your picture it makes the casting person angry. An angry casting director is a bad thing. They will remember you negatively.

DAVE NAVARRO

Quite a while ago, Dave Navarro came to me for pictures. He was an up and coming, gorgeous, talented guitar player.

Very humble, nice. I had no idea what a monster talent he was would become when I shot him.

It was great to see him succeed with bands such as The Red Hot Chilli Peppers and Jane's Addiction. Wonderful to see him starring on "Rock Star® with INXS.

To this day I sincerely hope my pictures helped him get big gigs.

I lost all my archives in the Northridge earthquake; so unfortunately, I personally have no record of the pictures. Maybe Dave has a copy. Hope to get a copy of that picture someday.

THE ACTOR'S RESUME

THE ACTOR'S RESUME

On a beginning resume put every theatrical job you have ever done. Put film work first.

Prior to securing an agent or manager, put yourself as the contact and be sure to list your coach. That is the most important piece of information on the resume, as most agents and casting directors will not consider an actor that does not have a coach.

STARMAKER MACHINERY

HOW TO BUILD A RESUME

Contact your local colleges and Jr. Colleges. Make flyers with your picture for the film department bulletin board. On the flyer indicate that you are willing to work "deferred". This means that you would get paid if the film is sold, but no money needed up front.

This is a good way to build your resume and develop lifelong relationships with upcoming filmmakers. Remember once upon a time Spielberg and George Lucas were students at UCLA film school. Just think if you were in one of their student films. What a great start to your resume!

Be careful to read the script prior to agreeing to do the part. Make sure that the story is not too "edgy" for your sensibilities. Law requires that if you are under 16 your parent must be within view of you at all times. Make sure you adhere to this rule. Shoots are long, arduous, lots of "down time". Bring lot to do. Bring drinks and food and a lightweight-folding chair that can be placed in the shade for each of your whole posse.

Your actor's coach may also be able to recommend you to some independent filmmakers. The larger you can have the resume the better. Remember, film agents hate to see an actor with a lot of live stage. They know that the actor will be overstated, hard to shoot and probably not book jobs.

It's tough. You can't get work till you've had work. But if you're creative and network like crazy with you acting coach and actor friends, and local film schools, you can achieve a good "beginner" resume.

THE ACTOR'S REEL

CREATING A GREAT REEL

The reel is what separates the novice from the pros. This is a digital video compilation of all the film and television work you have done. It doesn't need to be long, but it needs to show that you can deliver a line.

You can also start your own YouTube channel with all of your good clips on it. Don't put stuff up that doesn't show you off at your best. Go for quality not quantity!

Do not be tempted to put live stage footage on it unless you are aspiring to work on the live stage. Film and Television are figure skating, live Stage is football. They are two completely different worlds. If the casting director knows you are doing live stage, they will be afraid that you will be too "big" for film and television.

When you work for the indi filmmakers and college filmmakers BE SURE to get a copy of the film. Don't worry about getting the whole thing, just ask for a copy of your scene. A digital copy is fine. This they can give you right away.

If you wait for the whole film to be edited you may never get it. Even if you end up on the cutting room floor, the footage is very valuable for your reel.

Even if the film doesn't make it out of the can, it is still a CREDIT! Even if your scene ends up on the cutting room floor, it is a credit and can be used in your reel!

Sometimes you will have to make an agreement not to show the clip for a while. It's worth it to make that agreement to get that clip for your reel!

Take that piece of film and transfer it to a DVD. These days, most reels are digital. They are safer to store, and duplicate easier. Easier to put your scene on YouTube as well if you have clearance.

Buddy up with a film student and have them throw on a title with your name. Having a reel when you hit the agents will give you immense credibility. Most beginners don't even have good pictures or resume. You are really separating yourself from the herd with professional pictures and a reel.

STARMAKER MACHINERY

When you present yourself to the agent with a good coach's recommendation, pictures, resume and reel, you are telling that agent you are serious and ready to go. You are giving them the tools they need to get you work!

WHAT'S IN IT FOR ME!

Most people approach an agent with a "what can you do for me?" attitude. Forget that. Look at yourself from their side of the table. They will be asking themselves these questions:

1. Has this actor done any work?

2. Is this actor well trained?

3. Does this actor do workshop regularly?

4. Will this actor make me look good?

5. The magical phrase.

STARMAKER MACHINERY

Let's take the questions one at a time.

1. Has this actor done any work?

In the film business there's a saying: "You can't get work till you've had work, and you can't have had work till you get work." A quintessential "catch 22". Most reputable agents have as many as 250 actors on their rosters. There are agents who have as many as 600.

In consideration of this, what do you have to offer that is up to the level of the actors already signed to the agent?

Hopefully you have followed the advice in this book, and you have some credits on your resume. This will give the agent a comfort level that your actor can "book" a job.

2. Is this actor well trained?

Any reputable agent will insist you do a "cold read". The agent will give you an appointment to come in. First, the agent will talk to your actor for a minute.

If the agent is interested in you, you will be asked to review a few pages of script for five or ten minutes in the hall or waiting room. These script pages are called "sides". Then you will be asked back in the agent's office to do a "reading".

This is where those expensive coaching classes will pay off.

If the actor is a child not reading yet the parent will feed the child the dialogue. Young actors many times memorize much more easily than older kids or adults.

3. Does this actor do workshop?

Any reputable agent will not consider you if you are not doing regular workshop. If for some reason you get yourself to this point without workshop, they will generally insist you enroll with a coach they recommend.

Now this is completely different than the "talent boiler rooms" we talked about in chapter one. The agent makes no money from the coach. The coach will be a legitimate one with good actors to their credit. Your actor will be going to workshop with other working actors.

4. Will this actor make me look good?

Saved the best till last.

In the case of a child actor, the parent's behavior is a key issue.

If the agent feels the parent will be a pain, they will turn down the child flat no matter how talented they are.

If the parent aggravates the agent, the parent will aggravate the agent's clients. They cannot afford to loose clients.

STARMAKER MACHINERY

A book came out by Dick Van Patton advising parents to call the agent every day to ask what the agent is doing for the actor. This is the best way to get dropped by the agent!

Sure, Van Patton can do it for himself or his kids, or himself. He is a big money working actor he's putting a lot of food on the agent's table, and they don't want that to go away.

Realize; the agent's day is completely filled with conversations with producers, casting agents and directors. If you want the agent working helping you, you'll get it much faster by delivering a tin of chocolate chip cookies or cappuccino Jelly Bellys.

Don't get in your agent's way.

NEVER, EVER, call your agent during "breakdowns". This happens every morning.

The agent goes through all the casting calls, and sends out headshot links. The agent will tell you what time is good to check in. It is usually mid afternoon, at the end of the day, the agent is calling talent to book auditions.

If you are well trained, and you are pleasant to be around then the headshot and resume will go out. Become your agent's friend. Not adversary.

Instead of calling them and harassing them, volunteer to come in and help them get the breakdowns out, or bring them the high caff coffee!

Make their life easier, not harder.

THE LOBBY IS A MINE FIELD!

It is common practice for the receptionist to report to the agent, casting director of producer of inappropriate behavior by the actor while they wait in the lobby. You must be on your very best behavior from the parking lot on in.

5. The magical phrase.

The phrase an agent loves to hear is: "I am getting lots of work on my own, basically I need someone to negotiate my bookings."

What are they going to do, turn down free money? If you have guts and creativity you can find work for yourself.

Buddy up with the American Film Institute in Los Angeles; become active with the Motion Picture and Television Fund. Join Central Casting. Often actors hired as background talent will be given speaking roles if the producer and director like them. This gets you a SAG voucher. Enough SAG vouchers and you are eligible to join SAG. That is gold.

What goes around comes around. Be active in the motion picture and television community; get to know people. You will raise yourself above the radar.

At the end of the day, you will get an agent when you deserve one.

STARMAKER MACHINERY

If you want to save time, don't go to an agent until you have all your ducks in a line. If you come in the door fully prepared, fully loaded, the agent will be impressed and work hard to help you. This is a true case of Agents helping those who help themselves.

Remember this: an agent judges first the TRAINING and creative talent of the actor; LOOK is absolutely secondary. The exception being if they are just looking for cleavage or a big bum.

HOW DO I KNOW IF MY AGENT OR MANAGER IS ANY GOOD?

If an agent signs an actor without an audition that's a big red flag. If the agent asks for money for classes then they are 99% likely to be substandard.

Agents that need to give "classes" to pay the rent are not making money as an agent. Successful agents do not have time to give acting workshops. They do, however, want their roster to do high quality acting workshops every week.

The exception is the agent or manager that comes from a background as a coach, such as Ernie, Elain or Lori Lynn Lively. Elain and Ernie are a manager of very successful actors due in large part to the wonderful coaching they provide.

STARMAKER MACHINERY

If your agent sends you out on auditions where there are literally hundreds of actors this is a "cattle call". Many times these auditions are even publicized in the newspaper.

THE REAL AGENT

The real agent, the big time "top gun", will be sending you to auditions where you have a specific time to show up. You may read against thirty other actors, but it will be organized. You will have a specific appointment time.

You will be called in most cases close to your appointment time. If not, if there is a delay, DO NOT COMPLAIN.

Ask to see the book of actors the agent you are considering represents. You can check their website to see who they represent. Look at the pictures. Do they look like working actors, professionals? Do you recognize any of them?

You want the quality of talent on their roster to be at or above your quality.

Ask the agent how many actors they represent. When they tell you, check it out with the Screen Actors Guild. Legitimate agents have to keep SAG abreast of how many clients are on their roster. Be cautious of an agent with over 300 clients unless it is a very big well established agency.

Unless the agent has a huge staff, they will not be able to service you with the attention you deserve. You will have to work hard to stay above the radar amongst so many actors.

A legitimate agent NEVER charges a fee for representation.

A BIG NO - NO

DON'T JUMP FROM AGENT TO AGENT.

If you're not booking auditions, if the agent isn't sending your head sheet out, find out why and fix the problem.

It may be that you need to bring yourself to the top of the pile by being more visible in a friendly way. Not bugging them, but as discussed, dropping off cookies. Taking them to dinner. Helping conduct traffic on open reading days. Make sure you stay above their radar.

A good agent will help you build your resume. They will send you out for the low budget jobs their more successful clients won't take. That is a boon for you. Get there early, do the job. Every credit on the resume is worth money to you!

The first 2 years are the hardest. You will go on audition after audition with no luck. This is because you are a Johnnie come lately. You must persevere and keep the faith. All of a sudden all the casting agents in town will be familiar with your face. That magical first job will come down the pipes.

When you start to work and be more visible, other agents will line up like buzzards on the wire. If your agent is doing a good job - if you are getting nice roles and are very visible, then other agents will want you. For them this is a free ride.

Don't buy into it. Your agent is the one who did all the hard work getting you known. Respect that and stay loyal. If you jump from agent to agent, you will get a reputation for it, and no agent will work hard for you. They will figure you are likely to jump, why pound for your actor.

An agent will do their hardest work for the actor who they feel will be loyal and stay with them when it's a downhill slide to the bookings rather than the uphill climb in the beginning.

Shia LaBeouf was very loyal to his agent,
Teresa Dahlquist at the Beverly Hecht Agency. He rewarded her greatly for all her work for him in the beginning when he was unknown.

REMEMBER THIS:

IF YOU ARE KNOWN WELL ENOUGH TO ATTRACT OTHER AGENTS OR MANAGERS, THAT

MEANS YOUR AGENT OR MANAGER IS DOING A GREAT JOB!

If agents or managers are telling you that your agent or manager is not doing a good job and you should hire them, a large percentage of the time it's because your agent or manager IS doing a really great job They have put you way up above the radar, otherwise, no one else would be interested in you.

Be also aware, if an agent or manager solicits you when you already have representation, it's AGAINST THE LAW.

DO I NEED A MANAGER?

When you start booking a lot of auditions you may need a manager. Your coach may approach you, and ask to manage you. This is very worthwhile if the coach is already managing other successful actors.

If you are new to the business, a manager can protect you from common, costly mistakes.

If your coach doesn't manage, they may recommend a manager to you. A good manager is worth every cent you pay them. The will field all the calls from casting agents and your agent. They will make sure that you know where you are going, have your sides, and are properly dressed.

A bad manager is a nightmare. They will sign you to a long term contract, do nothing for you, and be there with their hand out when you book a job on your own.

MAKE SURE to check a manager out thoroughly prior to signing a contract. Ask them for a list of actors they currently manage and call those actors to make sure they are happy with the management. Hold out for a manager that has a good percentage of working clients. If you've never heard of the actors on the manager's roster then how good can that manager be?

Make sure the manager has introduced new talent, is not just a buzzard, living off the hard talent development work done by a previous manager.

Years ago I developed a band to the point they had a ten record label bidding war going on. A friend convinced me to move the band to a "big" management company. I did it as I thought it was in the band's best interest. Turned out the management company was just a buzzard operation. They had never been responsible for actually breaking an artist. Very sad.

A theatrical manager traditionally gets 15% to 20% of the actor's gross earnings. If a manager asks for more than that tell them that you are willing to pay 15%, see what they come back with. I do not advise paying more than 20% unless the manager is putting very significant monetary investment into you.

STARMAKER MACHINERY

The exception to this is when a manager is going to significantly fund an actor's career. In this case it may make sense to negotiate a percentage pay back for any investment, including interest, plus the 15% manager fee. So once you have paid back the investment you don't continue to owe the manager.

The contract with your manager should have an out clause. This clause should entitle the manager to continue to make commission on anything that you have booked while you have been managed by them.

If you move to a new manager they should ONLY be entitled to commission any ADDITIONAL monies they negotiate for you. They will not take the commission of agreements made by the previous manager.

This is a good agreement as it prevents a "buzzard" manager from swooping in and taking away the reward for the work your previous manager did. It will motivate the new manager to work hard for you, otherwise he will make nothing.

It also tells you that the new manager really believes in you and your potential elevated success. He is intending to make money from his industry contacts for you.

You should have the right to terminate the contract with 30 day notice if you are not satisfied. The manager should retain any commissions for work he secured for you during his tenure. If you terminate your management contract, there is usually a clause in it that says the manager is still entitled to commissions for any work they got for you while they were managing you.

The new manager should only be entitled to any new work they get you, or commissions for any raises in pay they negotiate for you.

In other words if you old manager got you a job that pays 100$ and the new manager renegotiates it to 200$ the old manager would get commission on 100$ and the new manager would get commission on 100$.

The entertainment industry is a very small town. Artists that allow their manager or agent to be screwed soon find themselves without a manager or agent and out of work!

WHEN TO HIRE A PUBLICIST

When you are booking jobs regularly it will be time to hire a publicist. The publicist's job is to "shop" the actor to press and media to secure interviews and personal appearances for the actor.

Blake Lively is particularly well represented by her publicists as is Kim Kardashian.

It's a loop really. A good publicist will help to raise the awareness of the actor and the raised awareness with get the actor more jobs. One feeds the other.

Publicists range from $700 to as much as $20,000 per month or more. Many times a long term arrangement can be made with a reputable publicist where you agree to a certain guaranteed time span such as 2 years. In return for this a publicist may give you a substantial discount on the fist few months knowing that they will be paid their full rate when you have more notoriety.

To get this kind of a deal, there has to be some "buzz" about the actor, otherwise, it's a hard job for the publicist in the beginning and they deserve their full rate. The less known the actor is the harder it is to get the press to write about the actor of schedule appearances. Ie: the more compensation the publicist deserves.

Literally every story you see in Media: TV, tabloids, magazines and newspapers, has been placed there by a publicist. Every appearance on TV shows has been booked by a publicist. Most of the guests on the daytime or late night shows are there because their (top notch) publicist has contacted the show's talent director and convinced them that their client will be an entertaining guest.

Once the actor is a superstar, the publicist acts as a buffer between the star and the people clamoring for appearances.

From this perspective, it is good to have a publicist that has a day to day relationship with these talk shows, etc. Unfortunately, the better the relationship, the higher the publicist's rate. And they deserve every penny.

Look at it this way, MacDonalds has used Leo Burnett Advertising Agency in the past to publicize their burgers. Now the contract, worth over 1 billion dollars belongs to Omnicom and Division of DDB. They pay them a lot of money, but the money is nothing compared to the additional people who are aware of their product. The additional sales justify the advertising.

It is the same for the actor. Instead of a burger the product is you. Your publicist is your advertising agency.

Your publicist has the same job. Make the industry aware of you. They will work with you to construct good, press worthy stories to feed down the pipeline.

These stories, if well written, will appear in media all over the country, even the wolrd, making a "name" for your actor. This name will get your actor more work, better work. It could make the difference between being runner up for the lead in a movie or getting the role.

SCHOOL FOR THE YOUNG WORKING ACTOR

When the young actor is getting his primary acting training, school will not be an issue. The coaching classes are after school or on Saturday. They don't conflict. Commonly they are once a week in the evening, 6pm to 8pm. This allows plenty of time to get the soccer match over and get to workshop.

Once a young actor is with an agent, and successful, that all changes. It becomes a scheduling Mensa test. Most successful young actors are bright; do well at school.

The exception to the rule is the "class clown". They are bright too, but they demonstrate it by comedic behavior and pranks. Not by grade average. The young actor will need to become adept at doing homework in the car. Once his career is off and running he will want to consider home schooling.

Generally young actors that are heavily working find home schooling much more efficient as they do not get behind. In fact many home-schooled actors graduate early and thereby are eligible for more scholarships. Colleges show preference to home schooled students. They say they come in more prepared to learn.

By law, when a young actor is on the set they must be supervised by a Social Worker and Set Teacher. There is much down time waiting for takes. During the school year this is spent in the film location classroom.

If the young actor auditions a lot and lives out of town, the parent will repeatedly have to take the young actor out of school to make the auditions on time. At this point you have to assess whether this career is important to the young actor or a passing whim. In the long run a young actor's education is imperative to their success in adult life. Any way you slice it, it has to work for the best development of the young actor.

This is another reason why it doesn't make sense to pursue an acting career if you do not really want it passionately. The young actor will miss many school activities, birthday parties and sleepovers. You have to Asses how bad he wants it. Is it worth what he's giving up?

If home schooling is indicated, then you call your school district. They will set you up with a curriculum and a good teacher. Many times the type of actor who aspires to a career in film also does extremely well in home schooling.

This is because to succeed in acting you have to be self driven. This skill is very important in home schooling as well.

A home-schooled actor can progress at his own pace, as fast as he likes. An aggressive actor can graduate years early. They can start on college extension courses and be far ahead of the game when they actually are ready to attend college.

THE CASTING AGENT RELATIONSHIP

When you are signed to an agent, the agent will start to submit your head sheet and resume link for auditions. ActorsAccess.com is a popular casting agent "goes to".

In marketing there is a rule of thumb:

The first time you see something you say, "I MAY do that". The second time you see something you say, "I WILL do that". The third time you see something you DO that. In other words, 60% of the return on an advertisement or promotion is on the third time it is seen by the same person and thereafter.

This is no different for you. Your head sheet and resume is

your advertisement. The first time a casting agent sees you, they consider you a "Johnnie come lately".

There are a million headsheets (aspiring actors) floating around in the entertainment industry. 99% of the "new" actors are ill trained, and have no working skills. From this perspective it is very unlikely that you, as a "newbie", will get a job over a similar actor the casting person knows as a well-trained actor.

The good news is that in the industry there are only so many good casting agencies. After about a year you will find that you know where you are going when you hear the name of the casting agent that has called you for the audition.

After they see you three times the casting director will begin to feel they know you. You have always been on time and have given good readings. At some point they will forget you are a "newbie" and they will give you a chance.

By the same token, the casting agent will start to remember your face. Most casual participants don't last more than a year, so all of a sudden, magically, one day you will click over from being a new comer to being a "regular".

STARMAKER MACHINERY

When I first discovered Margo Harshman she had no resume. She was competing with girls her age (10) with 6 and 7 page resumes. I got her a really good agent that believed in her. Then on each audition she took candy suckers with flags that said, "Thank You, Love Margo".

At first I think she just got the calls for the candy. She was good and now she does have the long resume.

Because you will see the same people over and over again, it's imperative that you maintain a really friendly face around them no matter how frustrated you are, no matter how long you had to wait. Ignore it when the same cranky actors or stage parent seems to butt in front of you at many auditions. As I write this Margo has the recurring role of Delilah on NCIS.

You need to be the "good guy", the cheerful actor. That is the actor they want on the set with the director. You need to be the "good" actor. You need to be the good guy! Being a "good guy" will get you bookings!

Believe it or not, there are times when a less talented young actor will get the part because they come attached to a "good parent". I myself am guilty of this casting practice.

Years ago when I was a casting director there was a blond fireman I always called when I needed the good-looking blonde guy. Not because he was the best looking. Hollywood is full of good looking blond guys.

I would hire him because he had a motor home, and he would always show up on the set EARLY with his pantry full of great snacks and hot coffee! He was always cheerful no matter how long it took. Kicked back in his motor home, no complaints. I always called him first.

That's what many decisions are based on. So it pays to keep small bags of "Thank You" Jelly Bellys in the car. Always have something extra to pass out at the audition. A smile, a thank you treat, they go a long way toward making sure that the next time your actor's head sheet comes across the desk he will be called.

Repeat after me, a cranky, pushy, impatient actor is a bad actor; a happy, patient actor gets the work!

THE AUDITION

What happens on an audition?

When you have secured an agent you will be sent on auditions. If you have a clear picture of what goes on, it can reduce stress.

First of all, absorb this! The audition usually is less than five minutes. You will go through a tremendous do rah getting cleaned up, driving through heavy traffic, not knowing where to park, frantically stapling your resume to your head sheet, rushing in, signing in, sitting around waiting, waiting, waiting.

Then bingo! Your name is called. You will go into the audition room with your sides (script) clutched in your hand.

In the audition room is a camera and a person sitting in a chair. The person is totally bored, they have been reading actors since 8:30 am and it is now 4pm.

They will read the sides with you and, if you're lucky say thank you. That means good-bye. "Don't call us; we'll call you."

The whole process will be five minutes max. You will spend all that adrenaline for a mere five minutes.

Is it worth it? One commercial can pay $10,000 dollars, more if it's national and runs forever. Adam Wylie's Dominoes Pizza commercial has run consistently for years. You know the one where he gives his new class pizza? That's a lot of college money. But the down side is that one commercial may take 50 auditions, identical to the one just described.

Let's look at the audition again, step by step.

1. Your agent calls, it's noon, they need you in West Los Angeles at 5pm. You live in Irvine, a 45-minute drive with no traffic. There are "sides" (a couple of script pages)

2. You call Showfax or Castnet. They say they'll fax you the sides. It takes forever, you're afraid they aren't going to come. Finally they do and you...

3. Being a really smart actor, you have several sets of clean clothes already in the car "just in case". Several different "types" that you go out for. In the car are also a hairbrush, makeup and plenty of Handi wipes to get all the dirt off

you as you drive to the audition.

4. You call work and let them know you'll be late.

5. You call your spouse and tell him he has to fix dinner for the rest of the kids and himself. He says, "of course dear, I'll be happy to!" Yeah, right.

6. You drive around for three blocks trying to find a place that's legal to park. You finally find a place with a parking meter, and being a very smart actor that has read this book, you get your stash of meter quarters and feed the meter.

Never, ever, park in the casting directors assigned spaces. Get caught doing this and you can kiss off any booking with that company.

7. Upon arriving at the audition location you try to remember which way the audition is and you trek off.

8. You remember you forgot your head sheet and resume. You go back to the car and get them out of a briefcase you leave in the car at all times with a mini stapler. You always staple at the last minute to make sure the right picture is showing.

If they want perky use the commercial. If not use the theatrical. The resume is stapled on to the back top two corners facing out. That way they can look at the other picture if they want to.

9. You find the casting suite. It is crowded with auditions.

There is always one bonehead giving the casting assistant hell about the wait.

Every so often a cranky intern will tell everyone to be quiet. Because you've read this book, you know to sit quietly and read a book. You know that many times they will have a TV monitor focused on the lobby, and your actor may be out of the running due to bad lobby behavior even before the audition.

You also know that many times the director will be sitting in the lobby as if he is there for an audition to check out the behavior of the kids and (more importantly) their parents. You will need a thick skin. Many times you will want to call actor protective services about "parenting techniques" you will witness.

10. You look for a sign in sheet. Make sure the sheet is for the audition you are called for. Many times casting suites will be reading for three or four auditions. Make sure you're signing in for the right one!

You will sign you name - time of arrival - time of audition and contact information (this will be your agent's name and phone number).

The sign in sheet is important. If an actor doesn't arrive on time for his audition, many times it is arbitrarily assumed he will also be late if he's booked. He's out of the running.

A cell phone is a must so you can call your agent if you're running late or lost. (Nowadays it is rare you won't have a cell phone. Make sure to always have a charge cord and plug.) They will call the casting director and finesse it.

Best bet; always arrive early. But even if you arrive early, do not sign in more than ten minutes early. Much of the time the person that is in charge of that particular audition is focused on another "type" earlier, and you will not get fair consideration.

11. After signing in, see if they need a Polaroid. If they do, an intern will be shooting Polaroids of the actors and stapling them to their head sheets and resumes. They do this to confirm the actor really looks like their headsheet.

Get this done right away. You do not want to be missing your Polaroid when your name is called. Make sure your coach has taught you exactly how to pose for the Polaroid. Commonly, actors that don't practice for their Polaroids end up with squinty eyes for smiling.

12. While you wait to be called, look around to get a feel of the competition. Ignore all the unhappy, cranky actors. They will not get a second glance.

Watch out for the actors that seem very relaxed, bright eyed, happy. That's your competition. That's how you need to be. They are the ones who "book".

If you are a parent with a child actor remember, kids are like doggies. If the parent is stressed and cranky the kid will be too. It goes "right down the leash". No matter how frazzled you are, don't let your young actor know. It will blow his audition.

13. At last! Your name is called. You, being bright and enthusiastic, jump up immediately clutching your sides (script) and head sheet with resume on the back, and go forward following the casting associate.

Don't have so much stuff with you that they have to wait while you gather stuff. You smile at the exhausted intern!

14. In exactly 2 minutes you're done. Elvis can leave the building.

15. You try to remember where you parked your car.

Ok, are you ready for fifty of those? One hundred? That's why you have to REALLY want to be an actor. To put yourself through that, if you aren't passionate, is simply nuts. Parents that make their kids do it when they don't want to, are doing it for their own ego. They couldn't care about their young "not wanna be" actor.

THE CALL BACK

The next day you're still getting over the stress of the audition. It's noon, the phone rings. The agent is excited; you have a "Call Back"! They want to see you again! Congratulations! You get to do it all again, except with call backs there will be less competition there. Same drill all over again.

You could get three call backs for the same job. Generally you will never hear from them unless you get the job. Get used to it.

Look at each audition as an event. Look at each audition as complete, in and of itself. If you're a parent and your actor is young, tell him that's the audition is the acting.

Let the far and few between jobs be a big surprise. A bonus, not the goal, the goal is doing a great audition.

Make sure you understand that you are an "AUDITIONER". Occasionally you will get to be an "ACTOR" Remember that every audition is a show. You're onstage. An audition? You GET to go ACT again today!!!

A career in acting is a career in auditioning. As an actor, you will spend most of your life auditioning. If you cannot take the fact that you will NOT get the majority of parts you audition for, you should= drop out. Otherwise you may turn to some kind of substance abuse to stay in the game. That's no life!

If you acknowledge from the beginning that you are an AUDITIONER, you will be much more likely to be able to take the percentages without going crazy. The truth is that you must do 30 to 200 auditions for every "job". Anything better than that is a miracle.

If you're determined to do it, find a career that will pay the rent and allow you the time to audition. Why do you think so many actors are waiters?

Most actors fill their spare time with workshops and improv companies. They make a rich circle of friends that they run into on many auditions. They become friends and work together for the rest of their lives. Many of the actors will go on to become filmmakers themselves. Your friendships are gold.

Sometimes you will get the job; sometimes someone else will get it. No rhyme or reason, just luck of the draw. It has nothing to do with the actors, it's all based on the whimsy of the person casting. The vision in their mind of what the actor they are looking for looks and sounds like.

Remember, each audition is a chance for you to make friends. Make it your goal to make friends and that casting director will go out of their way to call you to audition for every role you could be right for.

Also remember the casting director or associate is VERY busy. So don't take up unnecessary time. Just be friendly and PATIENT. The agent will remember you.

THE COLD READ AUDITION

WHAT ARE SIDES?

"Sides" are small portions of the shooting script. When the actor auditions, they will either be faxed sides, or handed sides when they get to the audition. If the actor is allowed to keep his sides, he needs to file them. You will then have them at hand if there is a 'call back". They are also handy to use at workshop.

THE MOST IMPORTANT THING TO KNOW...

When auditioning, never ever deliver the line while looking down at the sides (the script pages). Even if the line isn't delivered perfectly, the actor must be looking up at the casting director or reading partner. This is called being "off the page".

If the actor is off the page, that tells the casting director that actor has skill. Being off the page also allows the actor to put emotion into the reading while having eye contact with the casting director or reading partner.

To not loose place while being off the page, keep the finger on the line being delivered. Then after delivery it is easy to move the finger down to the next line.

This shows the actor is a pro and is not hard to practice at home with the parent.

WHAT IS A COLD READING?

Cold reading skill is what really separates the men from the real actors from the wanna-bees. You are handed a couple of pages of script on arrival. You have approximately ten minutes to learn it, and then you have to deliver it.

This is where all the workshops pay off. Every acting workshop of any worth will do a cold reading almost every session. By the time you will confront this you should be a pro.

You must be able not only to deliver the lines, but also be able to draw a character out of your bag of experience to use for delivery. Put some bells and whistles on your delivery.

I think a good analogy to a cold reading experience is standing on the platform of a subway.

The first time you stand there you are overwhelmed by the smell of fumes, the noise and wind of the train and the crush of the people pushing against you.

After you ride the subway to work for a week or so you can stand there juggling your Latte and reading your paper, tuning out all the noise and chaos around you.

It is the same experience in a cold read audition. If you are used to doing it you can tune out all the x factors, and truly focus on what you are doing.

Repeat after me... "Workshop is our friend!"

Do you remember your wedding? I've talked to many people who all say the same thing. "It was all a blur". If you had to get married every week, or every day, you would eventually settle in and be comfortable, able to focus, no adrenaline.

That's the frame of mind you need to be in at the audition. Just as the ice skater needs to have fallen on his butt time after time at practice, the actor needs to dial himself in at weekly workshop so he can truly focus and not be on adrenaline rush at the audition.

If you rarely leave your living room, are introverted, then you desperately need workshop. It will be scary for you at first, but the socialization and focus skills are imperative.

Just as a desert predator knows when an animal is scared, a talent agent or casting director knows when an actor is scared. Workshop is not only our friend; it is a must.

WHEN IS SCARED OK?

When I was a kid I was terrified of being onstage, but all I wanted in life was to be an actress. So I was willing to step over the line of my fear and go onstage.

Those workshops I missed out on would have given me the courage to pursue the acting.

From that standpoint, if an actor is an introvert, but passionate to be an actor, they must get coaching. Fulfill your dream!

JOEY PAUL ON THE COLD READ

Award winning Producer, Director and Casting Director and Acting Coach Joey Paul Jensen has been the casting director on more than 50 films and television shows. Her credits include "Even Stevens", "Hey Arnold", "That's So Raven" and "Soul Surfer".

MD: How important is it to deliver every word perfectly in a cold read audition?

JP: It's actually more important to show how you relate to the person you are reading with, and relate in front of the camera than to remember every word verbatim.

Many times in a cold reading an actor will completely loose the pace when he stumbles trying to remember the words. It's better to get the gist of what is being said and "fake it", improvise, if you can keep the energy going.

MD: What is the most important aspect of a cold read?

JP: Be **"Off the Page"**. In other words, when you are delivering your line look directly at the person you are reading with. It's ok to pause slightly to look down and get the line, but look up BEFORE you deliver it. Then react to the line from the other person before looking at the page again.

Nothing is less interesting than looking at the top of someone's head as they read their line off the page. In a "Cold Read" you are forgiven for not knowing the line, but you are not forgiven for reading instead of acting.

SUMMARY

Ms. Paul brings up a great point in being "off the page". Speed-reading and memory courses are extremely useful to an actor's war chest of skills.

A good exercise is to read to a friend, parent or the bathroom mirror. Have your partner stop you the minute you are not **off the pag**e. If you are looking at your partner or yourself in the mirror as you deliver the line, you are not reading. Go for eye contact.

Good actor's workshops put large focus on developing cold reading skills. Most audition calls are last minute with little or no time to prepare. If you do your cold reading workout every week, you will be ready when you are standing on the X and the light turns on!

The good actor works hard to perfect his cold reading skills. The brain synapses need to be developed so that the actor can absorb information very quickly. It might be frustrating at first, but give your brain a chance; it will develop the skill with repetition.

Develop the synapse for quick memorization; it will serve the rest of your life no matter what career ultimately you choose. It will be especially invaluable in attaining those sought after "A" grades that mean scholarship money for college, or those company promotions.

THE ICE COLD READ

The most feared audition of all is the "Ice Cold Read". This means you have never seen the "sides" (script pages) prior to stepping in front of the casting agent or director to read.

If you are well trained in the "Ice Cold Read", you have nothing to fear.

Being able to do well on an ice cold read is an imperative skill for the passionate actor. It will separate him from the novice. The only way to become proficient is to practice, practice, and practice.

Do it at workshop, do it at home, Use the newspaper, anything you can pick up and read aloud. You are allowed one pass. No going back. And you MUST be "off the page".

Don't be embarrassed to do it in front of friends and strangers. Read to people at the Laundromat. If you don't practice it like it will be, in front of people, you will seize up when you are doing the real thing.

Think of it this way, you can't learn to ride a bike by thinking about it, you have to actually do it. You have to be willing to fall. This is another instance where being well trained gives the actor an advantage. The actor's brain will be geared for learning, absorbing information quickly. It won't take you long to develop the cold read skills you need to excel.

YOUR READING SKILLS

Good reading skills are imperative for the actor. There have been successful actors who have had reading disabilities such as dyslexia, but they are at a severe disadvantage against the actor who is the avid reader.

When an actor is very young it is permissible for the parent to feed him the lines prior to the audition. Young actors are wonderful mimics; they will deliver the line back, usually with very close, if not identical inflections as the person feeding them the dialogue.

When the actor is in first grade however, even that early, he is going to be up against young actors with big resumes who are very capable readers. In second and third grade he will be penalized on auditions by his lack of reading skills.

FROM THE PRODUCERS PERSPECTIVE

Ethlie Ann Vare

Producer/Writer Ethlie Ann Vare ("Renegade", "Silk Stalkings", Gene Rodenberry's "Andromeda"), "Earth Final Conflict" and "CSI" makes the following observations:

MD: When an actor auditions, what interests you?

EAV: As a writer producer we have a specific image in our mind for each part. Do you happen to sound and look like the person we have in our head? That person gets the job.

MD: What turns you off most in an audition?

EAV: Being too "Actory", asking for a moment to prepare. Meditating before reading, doing 'actory things" like doing an exercise from actors class before reading. It's not good to seem too actory, serious or pretentious. We have to hang out with you guys on the set; we want you to be fun.

MD: What's the most important word of advice you have for a beginning actor?

EAV: It never hurts to do your homework. If you have an audition get on www.imdb.com. Search the producer or director, see what else they have written, directed or produced. When you go in to audition say, "I loved that movie.... how did you get that shot...."

Entertainment is a business based on personal relationships. If you know someone that has worked with them don't hesitate to say, "You worked with my friend so and so on such and such." or, "Hey I understand you know so and so." That will make the people feel like you're one of them.

IN SUMMARY

The most important point Ms. Vare makes is to be fun, be friends. Remember, the producer, director and casting director are people too; they are human beings, just like we are. As Cindy Lauper says, "We just wanna have fun."

There is no way to know what visual image the producer;

director or casting agent has in his or her head. If you are fun to be with, they will call you again even if you didn't fit the part this time.

I personally have even been known to create a part for an actor who read well and was fun to be around. Just take a deep breath (not too "actory" remember) hang your toes over the front of the board, and have fun.

WHAT DOES AN ACTING CAREER COST?

"Every dime you have".

An acting career is like any other business start up. Rule of thumb is a successful new business cannot expect to break even for two years. It is much worse with acting. If you start a taco stand, have good food and advertise properly to a two-mile radius around your stand, you will attract customers immediately.

In the acting business there are as many as 30,000 actors available for any part offered. In this business you have to be very well trained, creative and co-operative to even get into the running for the job.

The good news is that because of the odds, the fallout is phenomenal. If you can bite the bullet and persevere for two years, you WILL start to book jobs.

Meanwhile you will spend a fortune on gas. You will have an outrageous phone bill calling your agent and manager. You will have to have a cell phone on every minute at home AND away. You will need a RELIABLE car. You'll kill a beater car in the first four months of consistent auditions. You will have to get used to CHEAP food and RENT including friend's sofas.

You will be paying for pictures (150 -500 per photo session) head sheets (150 -250 per 100) workshop (150-250 per month), ActorsAccess Membership.

You may want to invest in weekly facials if you are prone to facial blemishes (20-150 per).

If you are a one-car family, you will have to buy a second car. You may need to arrange a reliable, last minute, no notice, childcare situation. A single parent cannot take a child to their audition. You will never book as the casting director won't book an actor who has "baggage".

A two-car family may have to become a one car and one van (camper) family.

There's no way to get around it; acting is costly. But so is any business start up. The problem is that most people don't realize that what this is. I know a young actor who has a 7-figure bank account waiting for his college years. But the first years were a real struggle for his single parent.

A vehicle you can live in rent-free is a really good

investment.

The more you do your homework, the better you invest in your career, the higher the likely hood of a return on your investment.

But the real question is. "Do you really want to do this?" ("Is this my passion or my ego?"

MANAGING YOUR CHILD ACTOR'S MONEY

Nowadays there are very strict laws regarding exactly what can be done with the money your child actor makes. Much of this legislation came out of horror stories of child actors in the past earning fortunes that their parents squandered. Leaving the young adult actor many times bankrupt, with nothing to show for all his years of work.

The Screen Actors Guild has a book on all the rules and regulations regarding the child actor. This is a must read for any parent contemplating an acting career for their child.

A certain percentage must be put in savings. On top of that your child actor will pay his talent agent 10%, his manager 15% and his accountant (if he's a big star) as much as 5%. Once he's up and rolling, he will need a publicist as well.

MEREDITH M DAY

CHILD ACTOR LAW

[10/12] New Actor Law Enacted In California

LOS ANGELES (Reuters) - California Gov. Gray Davis has signed into law a measure to bolster financial safeguards for actor actors, making it more difficult their earnings to be poached by parents or guardians, his office said Monday.

The measure, which amended a 61-year-old statute known the Coogan Law, requires that at least 15 percent of a actor actor's earnings be placed in a court-monitored account to which the actor would have exclusive access upon reaching adulthood.

Money in the trust fund is to be invested in "low-risk financial vehicles," with no withdrawals until the actor turns 18. The bill was signed Sunday, said a spokesman for the governor.

The set-aside provision previously applied only to actor actors whose employment contracts had been approved by a court, a circumstance common decades ago but relatively rare today.

The new law also stipulates that all of a actor actor's earnings be treated as "the minor's sole legal property," with parents or guardians considered trustees of the money.

As such, the earnings of underage actors are to be spent primarily for the actor's benefit, and parents can be held accountable in court for those expenditures.

"This gives the actor more legal rights to question how their money has been spent," said state Assemblywoman Sheila Kohl, a Santa Monica Democrat, who cosponsored the bill and is herself a former actress.

Previously, the earnings of an actor, like that of any other minor under California law, legally belonged to the parent or guardian, she said.

"My parents put all my money away. ... So I was very, lucky," said Kohl, who co-starred on the TV series "The Stu Erwin Show: Trouble With Father" 1950-55) and "The Many Loves of Dobie Gillis" (1959-63). ``I was horrified by some of the stories were told in the Judiciary Committee, which I chaired."

The original Coogan Law was enacted in 1938 in response to the plight of actor Jackie Coogan, who found upon reaching adulthood that his mother and stepfather had squandered about $4 million of the money he had earned as one of the highest-paid actor stars in Hollywood during the 1920s.

Ultimately, Coogan, star of such films as the 1922 silent version of ``Oliver Twist," was able to recover just $126,000 of his actorhood earnings.

Coogan was not the only actor exploited by his elders.

According to the entertainment trade paper Daily Variety, Shirley Temple ended up with just a few thousand dollars and the deed to her dollhouse in the backyard of her parents' Beverly Hills home.

The earnings of Macaulay Culkin, star of such films as "Home Alone" and ``Richie Rich,'' supported his large family until a court wrested control of the money from his feuding parents.

"Diff'rent Strokes" TV star Gary Coleman's parents structured his pension fund so that when it was dissolved, his share was $220,000, while his parents' was $770,000. Last Updated: 10/12/99 01:32 EDT.

MAINTAINING FAMILY SANITY

Having a child actor in the house is rough on other siblings. Make sure you don't loose track of them in the chaos of making it to all of your young actor's auditions. Having family support is imperative for a successful career for your child actor. A jealous sibling can be a damaging, even a dangerous/tragic scenario.

Rarely is there an audition on the weekend. Make sure to do special things for the other siblings when you are home. Don't leave them with "middle child" syndrome.

It is imperative to have the support of both parents. Many times you will need your spouse to fix dinner or pick up kids for you.

In the first year or year and a half, when it seems like Johnny will never get that first booking, they need to understand that his start up expense is no different than any other business. It takes extraordinary time and financial commitment.

Sadly, too often parents give up at just the time that their child actor is starting to be known by the casting agents. They quit, just as things are getting rolling for their child actor.

The road is a hard one for the family. Because auditions for school age actors are in the range of 3:30 to 6pm, many times the parent driving to the audition will not be available to be home after school or fix dinner. The whole family will have to turn into a well-greased "village". The first one home knowing that they must start dinner.

You should become familiar with all the "easy prep" NUTRITIOUS dinners available from places like Costco. You will need things that your family can "nuke" up for dinner if you need them to.

A co-operative grandmother can be a golden asset. A caregiver who is willing to be at your house after school till you get home.

In olden days there were always three or even four generations around the farm, now days we tend to be so insular that grandparents live far away. Busy with their golf games.

If your child actor is getting very successful (busy), it may be worth a move within walking distance of an amenable grandparent. Or, better still a move to a house with a "granny suite". So you have built in supervision when you are not there.

STARMAKER MACHINERY

If you only have two children and one is small, there is no reason you can't lug him his older sibling's auditions too, rather than having to do a baby-sitter. Be sure, though to have plenty of bottles and diapers. A screaming baby will kill your actor's audition quicker that you can blink.

Adam Wylie (Pickett Fences) started out as an infant being taken to his older brother's auditions and coaching. By the time he was of age to act he was very well trained. An award-winning actor today, Adam truly "grew up" in the business. He is very bright, absorbed everything around him. But more importantly, he loves performing. That's the key to a successful career for an actor.

I personally expect to see Adam Wylie follow Jackie Coogan and Ron Howard, and one day be a fantastic producer/director. Hope I am right!

No matter how much your actor wants to act, if your family is not supportive, you will not be able to persevere. At some point you will come to a crossroad. A choice. Stay with the family, or go with your actor.

In this case, forget the Hollywood thing, and encourage your actor to participate in every hometown acting opportunity. When he graduates from high school try to get him into USC or UCLA. They have world-class drama departments.

Remember your actor is only young for a mere 18 years. He will have the rest of his life to pursue an acting career if he is truly driven. Don't crash your marriage or family over it. Not worth it.

ON SET BEHAVIOR

It's important for actors to bring busy work to shoots. Every couple of hours you will work for two or three minutes. There will be times when you wait all day and don't do anything.

You need to bring plenty to occupy your time. It must be quiet stuff. If you are tapping away at a laptop, be sure it is away from the shooting area, even slight noises are picked up by the sound man, and it really pisses off the director and producer when they have to re take a scene because of an actor.

Screenwriting is a great way to pass the time. Buy the Movie Magic Screenwriter for you laptop, and who knows you could write the next blockbuster!

Generally "day players" (not the stars) that are not needed on the set are given a certain area to sit in, usually (hopefully) shaded.

As the day wears on, you will get bored and be tempted to talk to the other actors or parents. Eventually the conversation and laughter will ramp up, and then you will get the pissed off PA or AD (Production Assistant or Assistant Director) over there yelling at you.

This is a BAD thing. Everyone knows who is making the noise, and it means everyone will know whom not to hire again. It's easy to explain. The production is spending as much as $10,000 or more a minute on set. You crash a take by talking; you have just cost the production 30,000 to 40,000 dollars.

This is a BAD thing. Not good for an actor's career.

DO NOT WANDER OFF

Another thing the actor wants to avoid at all costs is to be "MISSING IN ACTION". Many times you will get NO notice prior to the director needing you. Things will seem to be dragging interminably, and then all of a sudden you will hear "TALENT!"

This means NOW! You need to be right where they asked you to be. YOU WILL NEED TO BE IN PROPER WARDROBE, HAIR AND MAKEUP. If you mess something up, get it fixed by the wardrobe or hair person immediately, so they don't have to fix it when the director calls for you.

If you're not in proper make up or wardrobe or if the PA

has to wander around and find you, they will MAKE SURE that EVERYONE knows it is YOUR FAULT, not THEIRS. Their job depends on it.

The actor needs to understand that there may be adjustments to set, lighting or sound that seem to be dragging on, but the MINUTE the shot is working they want the talent THERE, IMMEDIATELY.

DON'T TELL JOKES

Every person on a film, television or commercial set is crucial. There is no "dead wood". Every one of these people needs to be totally focused on their job, while at the same time keeping their "radar" going. This means that while they do their task they must also be eavesdropping on the people in the food chain above them.

The minute they hear that there is an issue that needs their attention, they MUST take care of it.

The crewmembers that are the most highly valued are the ones that seem to be psychic. In other words, before the director knows he is going to need something they are standing there holding it ready for him.

A simple example: The makeup assistant must be on the set watching closely, and before being asked, zip in and get rid of sweat on the actor's face.

Where an actor can really ball up the works is to feel like

"entertaining the crew". Most crew don't want to talk, and the crew member that will stop what he's doing and listen to witty repartee from the actor, or worse yet, the actor's resume, will end up fired.

Good crewmembers want their minds totally on their jobs and the needs of the director. They don't want to talk.

You as the "talent" do not want to be responsible for holding up the shoot. As I said before, if you do, the one you trip up will make sure EVERYONE knows YOU were responsible. That's a BAD thing.

ON SET PERKS

Every set has a "Craft Services" area. This area has drinks, candy, veggies, finger food, etc. It is meant to serve the talent and crew if they get the "munchies" before or after meals.

The parent of the child actor must be very careful, and set down rules at the beginning of the FIRST day.

Traditionally craft services have big jars of red vines and other candy as well as caffeine-laden soft drinks and coffee. If the actor eats and drinks a bunch of this stuff he will have a cranky come down. When the sugar and caffeine wear off, exhaustion will set in.

If caffeine is a pattern in your life, and you have to go without it, you may suffer from a migraine "caffeine come down". Inevitably, this happens at the exact moment when the director calls for you. You don't want this to happen, it is a BAD thing. You need to be cheerful, clear headed and co-operative when the director calls for you.

The best course is to stick to non-sugar, high protein snacks for the first half of the day such as fresh veggies. Calcium is a natural sedative. If you are on a sugar low, cranky or jittery, a glass of nice cold milk can calm you right down.

Late in the day, when you are exhausted and bored, then eat a few red vines to bring you back up, but save it till just before the director calls. If you are "sugar sensitive" don't do it. Sugar sensitive people cannot absorb commands when they are "High". The director will have to repeat the instructions over and over. You may blow your lines. You will not be hired again.

THE ACTOR'S SURVIVAL KIT

In the area the day players wait there are never enough chairs. You will want to be sure and bring your own folding chair or beach recliner and perhaps an umbrella if you are allowed to.

The "Honey Wagons", toilets, will stink, and they will run out of toilet paper early in the day. You are smart to have a roll of toilet paper and SEAT COVERS in your bag.

Successful working actors usually have at least a van. It usually has it's own little "Port O Potty." That is very handy on shoots where you can bring your vehicle.

Bring sunblock. Bring a large bottle of water in a sling you can wear. (You don't want to leave it around). Bring a sweater AND a jacket. If the shoot goes into the night it can get cold.

Bring Extra Strength Tylenol or Excedrin Migraine if you are prone to headaches.

If you are filming out doors, it's also good to have sunblock and an antihistamine such as Benadryl with you. It can bring down the histamine reaction of bad sunburn as well as bug bites and poison ivy. It's good to have a little first aid kit with stuff like Band Aids and panty liners. It's a good way to network with the cast and crew. Have emergency stuff available.

Bring a broad brimmed sun hat as long as it does not negatively affect your hair. You will even see male crew wearing these on sunny shoots. If you can't wear a hat, bring an umbrella. The kind that clamps onto your chair is a great one.

If you can bring your own car to the shoot, you can also have some alternative wardrobe in the trunk including shoes, hats and bags. This will make you VERY invaluable if they can get several "background people" out of you at the last minute.

It's very common that the director wants to flesh out a scene and ends up even putting crewmembers and parents in.

If you bring a cell phone, BE SURE they are BOTH set to VIBRATE. The first time your cell or pager beeps during a take will be the last time you work for that company.

NETWORKING ON AND OFF SET

The way to get work is to "network". Simply, this means make friends. Avoid the pitfall very common to actors of feeling that you must give your resume to everybody and talk about yourself. Years ago in an "EST." seminar Werner Erhard said something that I have found valuable ever since.

"If you want to be interesting, be interested."

This means people have more fun talking about themselves than hearing others talk about themselves (boring). In the hours you are on the set, LISTEN to others **DON'T TALK ABOUT YOURSELF**. Let others tell you about themselves.

Let the PA vent to you about her girlfriend. Let the star's manager tell you about his vacation in Cabo. Be a vacuum, LISTEN; don't be sucked into the temptation to "one up".

Don't try to verbally prove you also went to Cabo; don't talk about your car. Let them talk about THEIR car.

LISTEN, LISTEN, LISTEN! At the end of the day have EVERYONE sign your script and include his or her phone number. Build your "Rolodex"!

NETWORKING ON THE FLY

The best networking story I've ever heard is about a young musician who came to Hollywood. He knew that he would never crack the glass ceiling so he got really creative. He snagged a job as a waiter or bartender; I don't know which. He saved ALL of his tips. He lived on mustard sandwiches (maybe in his car). Anyway, he would dress up on his off time and hang out in the "power player" bars. He would LISTEN to people and buy them drinks. He became FRIENDS with the power players.

Out of that effort got a 3.5 million dollar record deal, and hangs out with celebrities. He's a creative, smart, hardworking guy, willing to sacrifice all for his craft. He deserves his success.

I confronted the similar glass ceiling when I decided to manage Margo Harshman. I had been a casting agent and filmmaker for years. I had managed and gotten a number of rock bands record deals, but I had never actually managed an actor.

What I did know was the whole business, whether music

or film, is based on RELATIONSHIPS. When Margo got her first role, a lead in a tiny indie Film called "The Elf Who Didn't Believe", I got to know Joey Paul the casting agent. We invited her to a fun event to thank her for the job. We've been friends ever since.

What You Give Is What You Get.

Too many actors only think about their own needs.

In any situation, put yourself on the other side of the table and think about what the filmmaker, agent or casting agent needs.

If you are hired for a low budget "Indie" there is a good chance the film will be looking for cheap locations. Perhaps your brother has a great old craftsman house in Pasadena. Talk your brother into loaning it to them. They will become your friend instead of just your boss. Perhaps your friend is dying to cater for movies, and is willing to do it cheaply, let them know, connect them up. These kind of relationships last, and are much more interesting than hearing about your acting resume.

RECOMMENDED PUBLICATIONS FOR ACTORS

There are certain publications that working actors read. The most important ones are Backstage West/East (East for the east coast, West for the west coast), Variety, and Hollywood Reporter.

All three carry valuable articles and audition notices. Hollywood Reporter and Variety carry production charts, which show that is working on what. If you follow these you can submit the head sheet and resume to productions starting.

Variety is weighted toward live stage as well as television and film.

Hollywood Reporter is geared more toward the film and

television industry.

Subscriptions to both Hollywood Reporter and Variety are expensive. For the beginning actor, having to decide on perhaps just one publication, I would recommend subscribing to Backstage East (east coast) or Backstage West (west coast). The publication comes out once a week and lists casting notices.

Even if you don't have an agent yet you can submit the head sheet and resume with the home contact number. All are available at bookstores and news stands.

HEADSHEETS AND RESUMES

Some actors prefer to print the resume right onto the back of the picture. This should not be done too far in advance, as there will, hopefully, be new things to add every now and again.

Prior to having an agent, list your personal voice mail on the resume. At first the head sheet should only carry the name of the actor. When the actor secures an agent, then the agent's info will also go on the front of the head sheet.

For a child actor, list the birth date, on the resume. Sizes and height changes too quickly. If you like you can list an age range your actor can play.

Personally, I like to leave just the birth day as the picture of your actor may qualify him for an older or younger role that may not be considered if there is a number of years on the sheet. He may look like he can play the part, but the resume says 10 and they want 8 years old, so they pass your actor by, when in fact he can play the 10 year old.

For the child actor do not list sizes; they change too often. If your child actor is booked, the wardrobe supervisor will call and get his up to date sizes.

Head sheets used to be traditionally black and white. Now, with the cheaper printing techniques, color has become popular. Your agent will have a preference you should respect.

If your actor has blonde hair, be sure the picture is representative and his hair looks light in the black and white photo.

Do not retouch the photo severely. The casting agent wants the actor to be the one who walks through the door. That's why they will ordinarily take a Polaroid as well in the waiting room. To verify the actor looks like their head sheet.

AUDITION RECORDS

The actor fills this out right after the audition. The best time is in the car following the audition, while your memory is still fresh. You can customize one to your taste, or use the form included here.

You need to make a record of the exact clothes, hair and accessories worn. If you get a call back, you want to make sure to wear the EXACT same wardrobe and hair. (If it isn't broken, don't fix it!)

You may not realize it; you are wearing the EXACT barrette that the director pictures the actress wearing. Yes, decisions ARE made on such trivial things.

You will also need to keep an audition and booking record. This is very handy for proving the tax deductions as well as an educational record showing the percentage of auditions to bookings.

This kind of an accounting can give you a very clear verification of the fact that an actor is truly an "auditioner". The best thing is to create a spreadsheet on computer so you can collate the information in a variety of ways.

If the actor is a great auditioner, occasionally he gets to act. I find it fun to list the actual bookings in color. (Red-letter days!)

You will want to keep a record of the following categories:

AUDITIONS - CALL BACKS - ON AVAIL - BOOKINGS!

I'VE GOT A SERIES, NOW WHAT DO I DO!

If you are so blessed as to get on a series the first and foremost thing you have to do is promote yourself. Typically the network will pump up the roles of those on the show that get the most "FAN MAIL".

Always carry a stack of cards in your pocket with your picture and your show's mailing address on it. As you become known, people wanting your autograph will approach you. Those are the people that will get you the raise and a bigger part.

When they approach you tell them thanks, sign the autograph, then pull out a card. Give them the card and ask them to write you. Many of them will, and that is what will get the network's attention.

"Work it Baby"

THE MUSIC BUSINESS

WHAT TO LOOK FOR IN A MANAGER

A good manager is very hard to find.

They must be impressed by the potential of your musical project. Impressed by both your vocal quality and your creative musical approach. They must also like the potential visual image. With the proper guidance, connections and marketing they should be absolutely certain your project could succeed in the "Big Pool". They will address the following areas in order to help your band to attract attention on the highest level of the Music Industry:

VISUAL IMAGE

They will oversee shooting pictures of the band. They will take both single and group shots. The pictures will be designed to translate the intensity of the music visually.

MUSIC

They should like your demo. They should feel it would make a good single CD or tape. They should be confident that it would sound great on the radio. They will connect you with services to record your CD if you need it.

RECORD LABELS

When the promo package is ready, and the band has a real buzz going along with a nice amount of "Indie" record sales or a significant number of digital downloads, the manager will assist the band in shopping the product to the record labels of your choice and theirs. With a good manager along with providing the right image, sales and buzz, you should get a good response.

MARKETING

They will oversee the finalization of a top quality demo package for Record Labels, Rock Clubs and Radio Stations.

RADIO PLAY

They will enable the band to access any time of day for musical exposure on the radio stations of their choice. They will also arrange for DJ support at the band's shows if the band so desires.

DISTRIBUTION

They will provide access to worldwide distribution immediately of the band's Cd if the band wishes to release an "Indie".

PRINT PROMOTION

They will arrange for reviews of the band's record in music magazines, and design print ads to support distribution if necessary.

FAN CLUB

They will assist the band in building a large fan base, both locally and in other geographical areas.

ENDORSEMENTS

They will assist the band in applying for equipment endorsements with major musical equipment manufacturers.

ABOUT BAND MANAGEMENT

HOW TO CHOOSE A MANAGER

There are two categories of managers.

1. FRIEND OF THE BAND
You may find someone who is willing to come to all the gigs and is able to watch over you, make sure you get paid, help promoting the band. Some award-winning managers have started out that way.

2. ESTABLISHED MANAGEMENT COMPANY

If you are doing very well at your gigs, if the "buzz" is out on your band, a manager may approach you. You need to carefully check out who else they represent, and their reputation in the industry.

If they say they have a close relationship with a record label don't hesitate to call that label, tell them the manager has given them as a reference. Ask them if they can verify they work with the manager.

If your manager is doing a really good job promoting you, then other "buzzards" will collect around your. They will tell you your manager isn't doing a good job and you should fire your manager and hire them.

Chances are that the reason they are interested in you is that your manager is doing a really good job. You need to immediately tell your manager about them and let him check them out.

There are cases where they may be from a large, legitimate management company, and your manager may be willing to execute a co management agreement with them. Do this only if they are willing to bring stuff to the table your manager isn't able to.

But be very careful checking this management out. Make sure they are whom they say they are and can really do what they say they can.

BUILDING A FAN BASE

In order to attract the attention of record labels or radio stations a band MUST have a fan base. The band must already have a "buzz".

This is not a group of close friends, wives and relatives that come to the gigs because they like you personally (or you make them come). This is a group of fans that come to see you because they are passionate about listening to your music. They sing along to your songs, press up against the stage and scream at gigs...

Look at it from the perspective of the Radio Stations or Record Labels. They are in the business of selling music, or using music to sell products. If they feel that a band has fans they can sell a lot of product to they will be interested in the band. The band has to show them that there is a large (sell out) interest in your music.

The biggest problem of building a fan base is exposure. If you are selling music, the potential buyer, i.e.: fan, has to be exposed to it.

Radio

This is the fastest, best way to build a draw. When someone hears you on the radio you're a star. You're three levels above local club bands.

Internet

This is the most dynamic marketing area available today. The band has access to many digital "music stores" that will sell your music. Get on a site like cdBaby.com and they help you market your product.

Visual Exposure

You must follow up radio exposure with REGULAR visual exposure. Many time fans are attracted because they think a member of the band is cute. They could care less about the music. Visual exposure also reinforces the radio exposure, telling the fan where to go to hear you live and to buy your CD.

Charity Benefits

Charity benefits are a great way to build a fan base. They are generally well attended, and you are not responsible for bringing the audience. It usually includes free media exposure for the band as well.

MP3s

While building your fan base give away as many MP3s of your music as you can to people who like your style of music. Your music is your ambassador; it will build your fan base. Now days it is cheap to share your music.

Local Club gigs.

Local gigs are a slow way to build. Each time you do a successful show, if your act is together, you will pick up a few fans. It's grueling and expensive. Social Media and Radio is a much more efficient way to build. What's better, playing in an empty club, or putting your music on the radio Saturday night and playing to thousands of potential fans? Or you can put a good video of your performance on YouTube?

Your Music

If your music has hooks and sounds good, and you look

good and are entertaining, every gig you do at a particular venue will be larger than the last until you are selling out. If this isn't happening, you need to diagnose the problem and fix it.

Your Songs

Keep a record of the most requested songs at each venue and on your social media. Make sure and play those songs when you play that particular club.

Fan Club

Be religious about fan club mailings. Now that is done online, in this era it is really cheap to reach all your fans instantly. Send out cool stuff at least once a month with a band calendar for the month. This includes what nights to listen to the radio, and which stations to call and request material. Always have a cool fan list person at any live event you perform at.

Have Fun

Above all, have fun onstage. Don't take yourself seriously. The fans want to have a good time. They don't care if your sound-check was late, your guitar's cutting out, your girlfriend's on PMS, or if they're the only two people in the club. They paid to see you to have fun and forget their daily life.

LIVE GIG DOS AND DON'TS

<u>DO'S</u>

Soundcheck

Do a sound-check whenever possible. No one wants to sit there and listen to you dial in sound; it makes you look unprofessional.

Be on time.

For both your sound-check and your performance. When you're a rock star you can be late on stage, when you're building your fan base you can't afford to do anything to piss off the crowd. There are too many bands competing for the same fans.

Go for the Babes and Boys

Do try to attract good-looking young girls (babes) and guys (babes) that will hang out in front of the stage. They will be a magnet for the club goers trolling and be very impactful in building your consistent draw. Your band will be known for a good-looking following. That's why a lot of single people go to clubs.

Hug Fans

Do acknowledge the fans with a friendly (non harassing) hug or pat on the back. Tell them it means a lot to you that they came. If you do this they will bring friends next time because you make them feel special, and they will want their friends to see that you dig them.

The Merchandising Table

Let the steady girlfriends or wives participate. Have them run your merchandising table if they look hot, are friendly and can make change. Sell T-Shirts cheaply so they're out there working for you. Give away stickers. Kids love stickers.

If your significant other tends to be jealous, leave them home. Remember you will only sell your music if you seem to be accessible. Remind your significant other that your job is to entertain; there is some fantasy involved there. Let it be.

DON'TS

Don't act out the fan's fantasy.

When you date your fans you will decrease your draw. As long as they have the fantasy of riding off into the sunset with you they will be at EVERY gig. When you do a one-night stand, and the fan knows it's over, or worse yet they find out you're human and have rotten breath in the morning, they will not come to see the band anymore. They need the fantasy, need to have you on a pedestal to relieve their 9 to 5 life.

Worse yet is the fan who, after a one night stand, will become a psychotic nightmare, pursuing you. If you start regularly dating a fan, then they may no longer feel like bringing their Babe friends with them to your gigs out of jealousy. Once again you will loose potential draw.

No Girlfriends, Boyfriends Or Spouses In The Front!

The most common mistake bands make is allowing girlfriends, boyfriends and spouses to hang all over them at the gig. <u>NO</u> singing the sexy ballad to your girlfriend in the front row.

BFF's in the front row turn off all the other girls (or guys) who are in fantasy about you. If your mate isn't comfortable being discreet in the club, have him or her stay in the dressing room. Most <u>smart</u> girlfriends or boyfriends stay in the rear of the club so they can keep an eye on things, but the fans don't know they're there. They understand that it's not cool to hang on you during the gig.

Don't allow a surly mate anywhere near the merchandising table. They'll kill off your draw.

Music Is A Job

You must NEVER FORGET YOU'RE AT WORK. If you worked at the phone company would you allow your mate to come in and hang all over you when you work? If you are smart you would not. It's even worse when it happens at a gig. Potential fans that think you're cute will be put off and go away. If they don't see anyone hanging all over you they fantasize about you and will come to every gig with their friends. Always greet them with excitement and give them a big hug. Remember though the minute you follow through on their fantasy and they find out you are not going to sweep them away, they will be gone.

You must explain to wives and girlfriends that you are at work, it is your JOB to attract fans. That's what fills up the bars and accounts for the bar tally.

The better you attract the fans the more draw you will have and the more you will be paid. Girlfriends that cannot handle a musician's job usually become Ex Girlfriends, or the musician becomes an Ex Musician - A or B check one. At the end of the day your job is really to sell liquor.

Sell the bar out of beer and you can name your price!

LIVE SHOW GUIDELINES

1. VOCALS - PITCH

If you can't hear yourself you will sing off key. If your stage wattage is higher than the wattage of the PA <u>YOU WILL NOT HEAR YOUR VOCALS</u>, nor will the audience. The most common mistake bands make is playing at a stage volume more powerful than the PA volume. This is generally instigated by "garage band" guitar players who like to feel the power coming directly behind them from their amp. They're not used to the power of a good mix, and they traditionally sacrifice the good of the band's sound to their own misplaced ego.

These days you can use auto tune at your gigs if you

wander on and off pitch. Use it if you need to.

HOW TO HAVE A GOOD CLUB MIX

Every club's PA is different. **The basic rule: To get good vocal sound the overall levels must be set at half the top decibel, or watt capability of the PA.**

A. Get a decibel meter from an electronics store.

B. At sound check have the sound engineer put the vocal faders at the 1/2 way mark. Without other instruments sing through the mike and measure the decibel level on stage.

C. Mike the drums. Pad the drums. Duck tape strips of foam inside the drums until they also match the level of the Vocals.

D. Mike ALL the amps. Play each instrument without vocals. Match the decibel level of the Vocals through the PA with each instrument.

Once everything is dialed in at half power the sound man can crank it through the PA giving the band a powerful, radio quality mix throughout the club. He will still have room to push each featured artist when their solo comes up.

E. At sound check the most important thing to check is whether you can hear yourself in your monitors.

The soundman will get your room mix; you must focus on your monitor mix.

IF THERE ARE NO MONITORS

If there are no monitors on stage each vocalist must wear an earplug in one ear. This will allow you to hear your head voice and stay on pitch. If you can't hear yourself your harmonies will be off pitch, which sucks.

If you have problems with pitch or power see a vocal coach. A specialist, not just a Seth Riggs type. That is the most important item to fix prior to shopping a deal. The best one on the west coast is Suzanne Keickle in Studio City (818) 769 5880. ($100 for first session $50 for subsequent 1/2 hours)

2. METER

Bad meter is a real red flag to A&R and producers. It costs money in the studio. Many times the drummers are simply replaced for the recordings. Bad meter on recordings is a nightmare for punch ins and for synching a video. The drummer must always play to a click track.

Get the kind of metronome that hooks to the belt and has earphones. Get an AC cord for it. Only use it on batteries only at the show. Be sure to have fresh batteries at each show. If you don't perform with a click track tape the show and check it against a click to see how close it is, it's usually a real wake up call, even for the best drummers.

Tape the show so you can play it back and check meter. When you're at a big show drummers are playing to a click. They're men not boys.

3. DON'T DRINK AND SHREDD

What you are doing on stage requires more precision and co ordination than working with power tools.

GARAGE BANDS DRINK WHILE THEY PERFORM. Even in his most heavy partying days, Joe Walsh didn't get high before a show so he's totally on top of it onstage.

You have to choose, music as a business, or music as a back yard barbecue hobby. You may have the chops, but when drinking, the playing gets sloppy, the pitch is off and the time suffers.

Drink all you want when you come off stage, but play sober or you better have some shredding hooks because you won't get signed on your performance.

There are substance-abusing bands that have made it, but they've made it on extremely strong hooks, heavy financial backing, their looks and the quality of their producer, not their musical performance.

4. WARDROBE:

When choosing wardrobe remember, you are an entertainer. Extend that to every aspect. Make sure the wardrobe matches the vibe of the project; think young. Remember youth is the majority of the record buyers. They're not going to be interested in a band that looks like their parents.

5. CHOREOGRAPHY

Don't just stand at the mike and sing. Move; play with the audience. Make sure you record video of your rehearsals. Keep what looks good; fix what doesn't. Watch lots of your favorite bands, whatever. Steal the moves you like.

Every member should play forward and have audience eye contact, that's how you build a draw. Don't just play to each other; you can do that in your garage. You are there to ENTERTAIN. If you're going to group together, do it but do it forward, include the crowd

THE AUDIENCE LOVES TO FEEL NEEDED.

Watch lots of live shows. Steal the good moves. Study successful front men, not the newcomers, study the perennials, the twenty year wonders. Study how they move and interact.

Watch when the audience reacts, that tells you what's cool. Study where they place themselves during the set. When you drop to the stage or the floor, be sure it's in a place you are lit and can be seen, or do something else.

Practice perching on top of the floor monitors if it matches the energy of your music.

6. LIGHTING

STAY IN THE LIGHT WHEN DOING COOL STUFF!

A common performance failure is not identifying spotlight placement. Many times a soloist will perform in the dark with the stage spot behind him. This tells the industry the band is inexperienced. NEVER solo or do cool stuff out of the light.

At sound check put duct tape on the stage where the "sweet spots" are so you can be in one when you're doing something cool. Worst case just position yourself so the light is in your eyes, that way you know you're lit.

If you're a musician, be sure the light is at least hitting your instrument and hands. Otherwise you might as well stay home and watch TV. When you work in the dark it really pisses off the audience. If the clubs can't light you, bring your own lights. It's easy to build a custom, compact portable light rack for club gigs.

7. SONG HOOKS

The true test of a hook is if someone (who is not in, or related to the band) can remember the hook and sing it after only <u>ONE</u> listen. Anything else is an "album cut".

To test a song hook, have someone (not an ass kissing relative or friend) listen. Play them three songs. Ask them which one they remember and why. Ask them to sing the hook (whether it's musical or lyrical doesn't matter). If they can't do this <u>easily</u> keep working on the song.

The other true test of a hook is when, <u>at every show</u>, more than one person requests the <u>same</u> song. Or before the show fans will ask you if you're going to play the song. Or you sell out of tapes at gigs. Or you sell out the shows. Or you sell out product in the record stores. Then you know you have hooks.

8. SUCCESS

How to create the magic.

Success is when people are calling the band up asking when they are going to play next, rather than the band having to beg people to come out. Success is over 100 <u>walk-ups</u> at the door at a local show. Success is selling out of product in the record stores as soon as it's delivered.

Success is producers, managers, agents and record labels bidding for you, CHASING YOU. Telling you to fire your manager and hire them.

Success is a $2,500,000 record deal, not a cursory end of the year cheap signing that doesn't include adequate development, promotion or marketing funds.

In this day, a record label wants to see at least 50,000 fans on the band's social media sites before they even consider the band investment worthy.

9. LIVE SHOW SUCCESS:

If the hooks are working and the image, energy and musicianship are in place, **each show will triple in attendance** until a local show SELLS OUT WITH A LINE DOWN THE STREET.

Until you can do that, you are a garage band. You need to identify what's still weak, and fix it. It's one of four things: A. Hooks, B. Image, C. Live performance, D. Recording quality.

10. THROW AWAY SHOWS

There is no such thing as a "throwaway show". The venue might look small and shitty, the sound may suck.

Something always goes wrong. The club owners may have made mistakes, but there may be important people in the room.

Everyone who is in the club, whether it's two employees or a packed house, will tell others about your performance.

A&R Scouts ALWAYS come out to see a band new to the area. The club may look empty, but that one person in the back, who doesn't seem to be paying attention to the band at all, the one joking all during your show with the bartender, may be a scout for a record label or a TV show. Everyone at the show will tell others about you, the positive AND the negative.

It's not uncommon for a good scout to know the caliber of the band after just a song or two. Don't save the best for last or you're screwed. Front load the set with your strongest song. It's not against the rules to do a piece of it again near the end. ***The rules are there are no rules!***

11. BAND ATTITUDE

As you know, the music business is a very small town. Every comment, whether negative or positive, has a long afterlife.

Keep all interactions positive. Restrict the bitching and the grumbles to the privacy of your own bathroom. Spew to your mirror, not in public where your invective can come back and bite you in the ass.

Professionals don't like to work with crybabies that can't handle the turbulent nature of the music business. A mike always goes out. Sometimes the power cuts off or an amp may crash.

Many times another band will be obstructive. Some times a great show will bomb attendance wise. You must remain on an even keel, roll with the punches, until you've earned the right via record sales to demand the "brown M&Ms".

ALWAYS be having a great time and let the audience (all one of them?) know it's GREAT to be there with them!

12. CLUB ETIQUETTE

Be the hero of the gig.

At every show tell the other bands how much you enjoyed playing with them, even if you thought they sucked. They'll suggest you for more shows.

Try to watch and support the bands that come on before and after you, this will encourage them to do the same. Even if you're busy loading out, take time out to tell them how great they sound.

Keep derogatory comments to yourself, they always get back to the band.

Every club has problems, ignore them and thank the owner or manager for the gig. If the problems were big don't book there again.

13. GIG SECURITY-ROADIES

When a band gets popular it's not uncommon for other bands to try to mess them up. This happens primarily by a good cord being substituted for a bad one, or equipment disappearing. Trustworthy road crew is imperative. They must stay with the equipment and make sure no one "twiddles the knobs" between sound check and the show. It's a good idea to tape the knobs after soundcheck.

On tour a good idea is to chain the equipment truck to a lamp pole by the axle (An Aussie road crew trick). Bigger tours assign a crewmember to sleep in the truck.

ABOUT THE SONG

Never record a song that hasn't been tested live. A common mistake of novices is to write a song and rush into the studio to record. When this is done the lyrics don't flow and the arrangement hasn't been tested.

You should not record a song until it's so tight you can perform it puking with diarrhea. You can't be an effective entertainer if you're trying to remember what lyric or lick comes next.

YOUR VOCALS

Your voice is your instrument.

The vocalists should drink only warm water in the studio (or at gigs). Cold beverages (and speed such as cocaine) cause the throat to tighten up and you will sing sharp. If the artist is too relaxed (alcohol, Pot etc.) you will sing flat and out of time.

Make sure you can hear your voice in your phones. Even if you're working with a famous producer, and feel intimidated, make sure you have a good headphone mix.

Even if the producer is recording you "dry", he can still put a little reverb on your voice in your phones. Don't hesitate to ask for it if you want it.

Most really good producers record the vocals "Dry" with no effects. Once they're on you can't take them off. Dry you can do anything you want in the mix.

TRACKING THE SONG

<u>NEVER</u> allow the drums to be recorded out of time. It's the first thing A&R and Radio listens for. If your drummer can't play in time (Many live drummers

can't), don't hesitate to bring in a session player to lay down the percussion.

Your drummer will still play the live gigs, but he could cost you a signing if he lays down a track out of time. Or worse yet, you will blow your studio budget trying take after take till he gets one in the right time by accident.

All drummers will tell you they can play to a click track, many great live drummers can't. To play to a click right you have to be used to it. Most live drummers aren't.

YOUR MIX

If something bugs you, tell the producer (or engineer) right away. If they don't have a rational explanation for it, one that makes sense, have them fix it.

Once someone buys a record it is usually played as background music as the listener does something else. The mix should be assessed at <u>LOW</u> level. Novices go into the booth and crank it. The trick to a good mix is if everything is present and accounted for at very low, almost inaudible level. Anything can sound fat on 11, what does it sound like on 1!

MEREDITH M DAY

NEVER do a final mix the day of tracking. Do a rough mix at the end of the day and take it home to listen to overnight.

Make notes of things that bug you, no matter how small. Allow the producer to bring up his mix without you there.

Make a file of your engineer's mix BEFORE you start having him change things. Always save each mix as a separate file. When you listen later with fresh ears you may like a different mix best.

Come in with fresh ears and assess the mix. Make changes.

Don't mix for more than 4 hours at a time; you will loose your highs or lows, especially if you work at high volume levels.

The final mix should sound good with all instruments and voices. You want an even blend at an almost inaudible level. If this is true you have a great radio mix.

YOUR PRODUCER

When hiring a producer listen to their work. Make sure they have credits (PREFERABLY GOLD OR PLATINUM RECORDS) that impress you. If the producer is young with no credits, make sure their recordings blow you away. Make sure they sound good on really low volume.

There are many cheap studios that come with engineers, but the garbage in garbage out rule always prevails. If the engineer doesn't know how to mike a drum, you will not get a good drum sound no matter how great your chops are, or how much you try to "fix it in the mix".

Realize that when the engineer says they are going to bounce tracks, they CANNOT BE UNBOUNCED. With Digital, Pro Tools studios this is not a problem since you have infinite tracks.

Once everything is dialed in, do a test run. Record something, pull up a rough mix and compare it to one of the cuts of your favorite artist. How does it sound technically? It is clear, fat and crunchy or a pile of mush?

Try to engineer the cd so that you do not have to adjust volume between the verse and chorus and between two tracks.

SUMMARY

This is your project. Your name is on it, and you will be sitting with industry when they listen (hopefully). If something bugs you, FIX IT! That will always be the first criticism you hear from the big guns. Trust your instinct. Don't be embarrassed after it is final.

LYRIC WRITING GUIDELINES

From MEREDITH DAY & the late GAYLON HORTON (Manager/Joni Mitchell, head of the Pop Music publishing division for the Welk, Music Group, President of Vogue Music Publishing, President of the California Copyright Conference and Chairman of the National Music Publishers Forum.)

Long ago Gaylon Horton taught me how to write music Lyrics. I am so grateful for his kindness. He thought I had talent, but said to me, "you have no concept of song form." Instead of getting mad and stomping out of his office, I asked him, "What is song form." Thank God I did.

Gaylon taught me about writing lyrics:

A. The syllables in <u>line 1</u> of <u>verse 1</u> need to be the <u>same as</u> the syllables in <u>line 1</u> of the <u>other verses</u>. This is the most common mistake made by lyric writers, and causes them to not be able to deliver all the verses with the same vocal power.

B. Don't stuff a lyric on every beat. Leave air around the words, room for expression, passionate delivery. THINK OF THE LYRIC ALSO AS PERCUSSION.

C. Get rid of unnecessary words such as "I'm", "Your", "and", "but", "so", "that". Use the least amount of words needed to convey a thought.

Example

Before:

"I really love you but you won't give your love to me"

"I feel trapped in love, I wish you'd set me free"

After:

"Love you... you won't love me"

"Trapped in love...set me free"

Before

"I'm tired of working in the city, no one cares if you live or die"

"I'm headin for the country, tryin to find empty sky"

After

"Tired of the city...who cares if you live or die"

"Headin for country...gotta find empty sky"

Same thoughts, but now there is room for music, hot licks and expression. Let the music surround and caress the lyric.

Exercise

Go through every one of your song lyrics and cross out every word that's unnecessary.

D. Leave plenty of room to breathe; the song isn't a track meet. Let the audience absorb each thought. If the thoughts come too fast and furious the audience gets lost and looses the thread of the song, or they just ignore the lyric, and groove to the music.

E. Think of your song as a painting:

Be sure to include space for lyrics, space for music and space for licks.

STARMAKER MACHINERY

PUMPING THE GIG

GET YOUR HUSTLE ON!

A band must be very creative when hustling for a gig. Remember, everyone has a buddy in a band.

Social Media is the main place to gather fans. The first thing a promoter or record label will look at is how many followers you have on social media.

The minimum amount of fans considered impressive these days is 50,000. If you don't have that, you are not considered a good investment.

GOOD TROLLING:

1. **Give away tickets to the gig on the radio and your social media.**

Overnight radio spots are cheap and they are available to local bands. Some stations even have a reduced rate for bands that are local.

Listeners that hear your music on the radio do not track it is an ad. Just hearing you on the radio makes them think you are cool.

The listener that likes your music will call or email for a ticket. This is a great way to build your fan base. BE SURE TO GET EMAIL ADDRESSES! Email addresses are gold. Always have a person wandering with a mailing list clipboard at gigs and anywhere else you can make friends.

In this web age, you are judged more by how many followers you have on your social media than how many people are at your gigs.

2. **Shopping Malls adjacent to the gig on Saturday and Sunday midday.**

Troll the mall. If you see a girl/guy smiling at you, they're interested, give them a pass to the gig, they'll bring a friend or two. Don't bring your significant other unless they are good at getting you fans. You will be less likely to be approached if you have your BFF with you.

Most young working types hang out and shop from boredom. You can tell the ones who'd like your music. Go to the movie area. Give away passes to people coming out of the movies. Pick movies you're fan base would like.

You know which malls the kids hang out in. Go there. Remember, now kids are less likely to go to club shows. Do a playstation giveaway at your show and pu that on your flyer. Never give it away until you are done playing. If you give it away early you will loose your audience.

More important, really work your Facebook friends in all the areas where you perform live. If they think you like them, they will come out to see you play.

2. **Other band's gigs.**

Support them and they will support you. Get to know bands in La. Cut a deal with them. They loan you their fan base list in their home town and you will help them get gigs down here and loan them your local list. Goes around comes around.

3. **Fraternity and Sorority Rows at colleges.**

Hang out Saturday afternoon; pass out free show tickets (with giveaway). In Los Angeles hit USC Frat row and UCLA Frat Row. Hang out in the cafeteria. Great trolling.

4. **Forget about your friends.**

Your friends are the best way to determine if your band is good. If your band is great, they will be begging for free tickets and volunteering to help at gigs. If your band sucks you will have to beg them to come out to hear you play, and they will leave immediately after you play. They won't hang out with you. Many times they won't even applaud if they are just doing it as a favor.

WHAT IS YOUR JOB AT A SHOW?

Remember, your PRIMARY job is to sell alcohol, that's why clubs have bands. They could care less about your music. If you bring fans who drink, you can suck and still book great gigs. You want fans that actually want to be at the club, will hang out with you all night, and will spend money.

It's not a bad idea to tell the bartender on the live mike, from the stage, that you are really thirsty and need a drink. This will cause others to buy more drinks too.

When scouting for fanbase, go for people who don't know you. They can be fooled into thinking you're a star. Your friends will jump on the bandwagon anyway when they hear your music on the radio.

WHAT DOES SWAG HAVE TO DO WITH IT

SWAG, the band or artist branded t-shirts, cds and other items sold at the band table are an important money maker for the band. The better the band performs, the more will be sold.

There are bands who sell enough swag to fund their tours. This is a great goal. A band I managed years ago, had no money at first. They would go to the thrift store and buy t-shirts for 25 to 50 cents and silkscreen cool stuff over the designs. They would sell them for 15 dollars! Lucky a band member knew how to silkscreen! Each one being one of a kind, they became a major band collectible as the band's following built.

T-shirts should be cool enough for fans to want them even before they care about the band. Be creative. Not just the band name, until the band is selling massive amounts of stuff. Imagine if the t-shirts said "I Really Don't Care, Do U?" on them?

Cds can be replicated for 1$ to 1.50$. These can be sold for ten to 20$. A great money maker for the band.

YOUR CD ART

Remember, when the band is new no one will care about your picture. Best to do something really creative that fans will want no matter what the music sounds like. Do something creative and topical. maybe find a really talented artist in your circle or at school, and turn them loose on your cd cover.

MOST IMPORTANT INVESTMENT

The most important investment a band makes is it's radio exposure. Brick and Mortar stations and Internet radio stations. Invest in both brick and mortar and Internet radio stations. Why do you think the record companies try to lock it up? Because they know the radio stations are imperative to sell music.

STARMAKER MACHINERY

Most people at radio stations barely make a living. Show up with Pizza and they will talk to you.

SEEKING BAND INVESTMENT

At one time or another all bands need to raise capital. The money may be needed to record new songs, or to do marketing and promotion. If the band is organized and has a clear picture for the investors of how they will be repaid, they are much more likely to attain the investment they need.

You need to be realistic. 99% of band investment is never recouped. Knowing this can be powerful. Do your fundraising in early to mid December. Approach your friends who are anticipating their tax returns and make enough to need write offs.

Let them know that your band needs investment. Tell them in return they will get t-shirts and music, but most likely the investment will be a WRITE OFF for them. If your friend needs some more tax deductions, that can be a valuable asset you have to offer at the end of the year. They have to give you their money before January 31st. You will give them a receipt for their taxes.

The investor needs to understand that they are participating in a HIGH RISK INVESTMENT. They also need to have a clear picture that they may never see a return on their investment. If you don't make that clear, preferably in writing, it can cost you a friend.

ABOUT YOUR PROMISSORY NOTE

Place the band logo at the top of your investment receipt for a professional look. Print the notes on nice paper. FedEx Office has elegant stationery that lends a nice look to an investment promissory note. FedEx Offices also has stock Promissory note forms. Again, be sure to specify on the note that this is a HIGH RISK INVESTMENT.

A licensed Attorney can draw up a formal promissory note. It gives the lender a comfort level that you are professional and they may get a return on their money. You will pay the attorney their hourly rate for this. It can be expensive. You can also find promissory notes on the web.

You will need to provide a signature place for each member of the band, the Investor, and a Witness.

HOW TO MANAGE PROMOTION

WHEN TO PROMOTE YOUR PROJECT

In the past it didn't make sense to promote an artist or band without a full collection of songs. Nowadays, with the Internet making it possible to have a song up and available to all the music streaming sites in as little as two weeks from release the rules have changed.

It is good to have a few songs ready. If the artist is good, fans will want to check out more than one song. Though for radio promotion it is not necessary to have more than one ready, an artist is best to have at least three songs. At the minimum an A and a B single (two songs).

Once all the art is done and the music and video is available online, the artist or management can hire a radio promotion company to promote the music to radio. Both brick and mortar stations and Internet stations.

This is not free. The better the promoter the more it will cost. There must be a budget available for radio promotion. In this era, large amounts of money are not made by record sales and streaming unless you are a major artist like Paul McCartney or Taylor Swift. It is made by live performances and appearances.

The money spent for Radio promotion is to raise the awareness of the artist, not for profit. If, with good radio promotion, an artist can make it onto the charts, this gives the artist value as a live performer. With radio stations playing their music an artist has access to better, radio sponsored gigs.

There are a number of radio promoters. A good place to start is Loggins Promotion in Nashville, Tennessee. www.LogginsPromotion.com. Run By Paul Loggins, brother of Kenny Loggins, There is decades of expertise there.

A "Blast" is also a good thing to do when the music is up on all the Internet sites. The blast goes out to all the radio stations the first week of release. It includes

Information about the artist and audio samples of up to three of the artist's songs.

If you are using a radio promoter, be sure to send them press releases as often as possible. Such as a release that your band or artist has shown up on a chart or is climbing a chart. Or a release about a personal appearance. The promoter can send these releases to their radio stations, reinforcing that your artist is worth watching and or playing!

SOCIAL MEDIA PROMOTION

WHAT'S LIKE GOT TO DO WITH IT!

In this day it is all about your project's "Likes". In the past a record company would look at the live show draw to indicate if a band was worth considering. Even more important they would have a guy by the swag table, keeping track of how many cds and t-shirts sold at a show.

These days the corporations who are now in charge of the music industry look at how many likes a band has. We are talking about 50,000 likes to even raise their eyebrows. Anything under that, you are on your own. You are a garage band.

The most common mistake that bands make when promoting themselves to social media is just showing themselves playing their music. If your band is performing in a club shoot the video from a position that shows a maximum number of fans. Remember. Fans attract fans.

Do not show bored friends or relatives that have come to your gig to placate you. Do not only show the band onstage with no fans in view.

Try to show footage of packed clubs. If you don't have a huge following don't play large clubs that will look empty. Play smaller clubs that will look packed with your draw in them.

If possible put up YouTube clips of fans taking about how much they like your band. Do videos of the type of fans that you want as followers, not your parents or auntie pretending to be fans.

FAN CLUB LIEUTENANTS

Get on Craig's list and hire some kids to be "Fan Club Lieutenants". You don't have to pay much, it's part time. Figure some affordable way to reward them for getting your band's Facebook page likes. It could even be pairs of movie passes for the lieutenants! Choose kids that have lots of friends on their social media.

Give them discount tickets to your gigs to share with their friends or give them a special door list to get their friends in at a discount or free.

STARMAKER MACHINERY

HOW OFTEN SHOULD MY BAND PLAY?

FANS HAVE A LIFE TOO

What bands many times forget to consider is that fans actually have a life. These days there is so much cool stuff to do between gaming and other pastimes.

Even before this hyperactive Internet Social Media environment, studies showed that fans needed at least three months to build a desire to see a band again.

If the band played more often than every three months in one geographical area, the fans burned out of them. "Oh they play all the time. We can always go see them. In other words, you are not special.

The best thing a band can do is to set up a circuit of clubs that takes the band to each area no more often that once every three months. The longer the gap, the more excited the fan is to see the band.

Big draw touring bands do one circuit every year or two. That way they fans are fresh, excited to see them. Your band needs to be special, not commonplace.

When playing a new club, try to open right before a popular local band. That guarantees that there will be potential fans there to see you. It also takes pressure off your band to fill the house.

Try to avoid the closing slot, as the fans that came to see the headliner will leave, hook up, get lucky, hasta la vista!

A headline slot is an ego trip. The opening slot is more valuable. Don't try to headline in an area before you have a local draw to support it. If you open for a popular band, the club will be full of fans that want a good position by the stage for their band. They will be belly up to the stage to see you. this is your best slot to build your fan base.

If you find your draw is diminishing in an area, that may mean you are overplaying that club (Or you suck). At the end of the day, always remember the reason the club will want you there is to sell alcohol.

If you don't bring alcohol customers, no matter how good you think you are, you are worthless to the club.

If you don't bring people, you won't make the club money and they won't want you there. If you don't make the club money, then you are not an "entertainer"; you are a club leech.

IDOLS AND VOICES - LIFE CHANGING

"IDOL" AUDITIONING

Because of the success of "American Idol", there are many spin offs, and many "Rock Star" type audition opportunities. "The Voice" has become one of the best singer tutorials available.

Getting seen on one of these shows really builds your following. It is a gold mine. Even the runners up get to do a tour with the winners after the show has aired.

THE AUDITION

When you line up to audition remember, all the competitions have scouts out looking at the lines outside way before you are actually on the hot spot.

STARMAKER MACHINERY

Even if you don't make the cut, there may be a powerful manager there with a client. He may see you and go crazy for you if you show off what you can do!

You will never know if the person hovering around you is an important "undercover' person or just another applicant.

At all times, you must represent yourself as a star. Even in the line, sleeping on the street, represent yourself. Dress like a star, act like a star. Don't save your good clothes and makeup till you get "in there". If you do you may never get in there. You need to own it!

This is not the place to be cranky or selfish.

Do not look down at your competition, this means acting as a true star and being the catalyst for the rest of the group. Make friends with everyone! Give them support and encouragement, they will pay you back!

Never be snarky or complain. I know casting directors who purposefully put the applicants into obnoxious situations to see if they will be easy or hard to work with. They will do this before you even go in to your audition.

It is common practice to record video of the lines and the waiting rooms. They want to know whom you really are when you think no one is watching!

If you have to wait in line all night, perform! Get groups of other actors to perform with you. Be the instigator. Have fun!

If someone asks you to sing, sing! Don't hesitate! You never know why they are asking or who may be watching from afar in a dark room on a video screen.

Adrianne Leon was kicked out of American Idol® because she was too young. But when she was warming up Randy Jackson was standing right next to her listening the whole time.

She didn't know who he was at the time. She could have reached out and touched him. If she had not been too young, I know she would have made the cut. Her handicap was she was twelve and looked eighteen. Yes 12!

At one point Randy asked her if she knew any covers. She was going to sing an original song for her audition. Though she knew every cover on earth, she looked up at him and said no, thinking I wanted her to sing the original song.

That was a bad mistake. original songs are much more expensive to get the rights for. That's why on the competiton shows, most often the performers will sing covers.

We should have had Adrianne sing a cover of one of the judges.

We all knew she was going to get kicked out for her age at some point. She did an academy award winning crying scene when it happened.

SONG CHOICE

Don't pick an obscure song. Research your judges; find out what music they like. Find a song they had a hit with. Pick something that went high on the charts, and they may have been involved in. You can find this out by searching their name on www.allmusic.com if they are in music. If they are in film, or do soundtracks, search their credits on IMDB.

Pick something that will really bring the energy up in the room and make people feel good.

FRONT LOAD YOUR AUDITION

Remember you may have only four bars, DON'T save the "Money notes". Hit them in the intro. Let the judges know immediately you are a contender!

No slow builds that bore the judges. They have a lot on their plate, they want to know immediately whether you have it or not. Give it to them immediately and don't be surprised if they let you go immediately.

You've given them what they need. Even though they may let you go quick they will call you.

You've blown them away, and you've done them a favor. You haven't sucked up their time!

GO DO IT!!!!

WHETHER YOU ARE AND ACTOR OR A MUSICIAN:

Don't bend with the wind, do what you like, what you will enjoy performing whether you become famous or not. That way, very worst downside is you'll have something cool in your life's scrapbook, something wonderful to show your grandchildren.

Doing something that inspires you will inspire your grandchildren. Leave them a great legacy. You won't wake up at sixty-five years old and then decide to do what you really like.

Do what you love and you will never have to work

MEREDITH M DAY

a day in your life.

GOOD LUCK WITH YOUR PROJECT!

"ME TOO" - HOW TO AVOID SEXUAL HARASSMENT

"Starmaker Machinery", is about teaching you the secret stuff no one admits to. Such as how prevalent sexual harassment is for both sexes in the entertainment industry.

Even with all the "Me Too" movements, the practice of enticing performers with promises of roles in exchange for sex goes on in all the dark corners of the industry as well as many other work environments.

In the entertainment industry, the "Casting Couch" has been an accepted practice for people in positions of power since the advent of film companies.

It is the performer that thinks out of the box who gets ahead. Avoids the "Me Too" abusive syndrome.

Sure, everyone will tell you what the secret RULES are. The actors who follow the rules disappear into mediocrity. The performer who is willing to go one step further with their creativity will find the secret door! A path to avoid the typical "casting couch" demands.

If a performer has leverage of either talent or attraction, they can get roles. If the performer is mediocre, they can sometimes get minor roles by using sexual favors. Generally though, this does not work. Many actors, both male and female, have hit the "casting couch" in hopes of securing a promised role. For the most part, the role does not happen.

Elizabeth Taylor was smart. You didn't get favors from her until you had given her the bling. She had the beauty and talent to be able to demand a high price for her attention. Paid up front.

One of the producers guilty of the "casting couch" syndrome was Howard Hughes. According to Harvey Prever's eyewitness account of numerous incidents, Hughes would have his limo pick up underage aspiring actresses with their mothers. The limo would park outside the back of his business offices on Sunset Boulevard in Hollywood below the studio of Paul Hesse and Harvey Prever.

STARMAKER MACHINERY

Their studio overlooking the parking lot, Harvey Prever and Paul Hesse had a bird's eye "bleacher" view of what went on below.

When the limo arrived, the mother was escorted into the offices and Hughes would climb into the limo with the daughter.

According to Prever, who did 3D lobby displays for Hughes' films, Hughes told him the mothers agreed to the "anything goes" assignations with Hughes upon the promise of a <u>possible</u> role in his films for their daughters. Prever was disgusted that the mothers basically sold out their daughters when they were minors. Only a small fraction of their young daughters actually got a role.

An actress came to me years ago and complained that all the producers wanted was her body. They just wanted to sleep with her. They never gave her roles, just promises of roles. She had a very famous producer she really wanted to develop a serious professional relationship with. Like all the others, he wanted her to sleep with him. She wanted a way out of this syndrome. This was a great work around for her.

I told her that whenever she went anywhere with him, to tell all those around him how brilliant he was, mention specific projects of his. She did her homework on his career.

Though he commonly propositioned other actresses, he took her everywhere and introduced her to everyone because it fed his ego. She ended up getting his attention because she was not focused on herself. She focused on making him important.

The bottom line is: the best way to get roles is to constantly do workshops like TVI and develop relationships with legitimate casting directors and talent managers. If you are a good actor, and professional in demeanor you will get the roles.

GO DO IT!

WHETHER YOU ARE AND ACTOR OR A MUSICIAN

Don't bend with the wind, do what you like, what you will enjoy performing whether you become famous or not.

That way, very worst downside is you'll have something cool in your life's scrapbook, something wonderful to share with your grandchildren. To inspire them. A great legacy. You won't wake up at sixty five years old and then decide to do what you really like.

STARMAKER MACHINERY

"Do what you love and you will never have to work a day in your life." Credited to Steve Jobs

GOOD LUCK WITH YOUR PROJECT!

Meredith Day

SUGGESTED READING

These books are very valuable reading!

FOR ACTING

Periodicals:

BACKSTAGE WEST

HOLLYWOOD REPORTER

VARIETY

FOR MUSIC

Periodicals:

MUSIC CONNECTION MAGAZINE

BILLBOARD

RADIO AND RECORDS

FOR OVERALL CAREER SUCCESS

"THE COOL FACTOR"

    By Del Breckenfeld

"PATENTLY FEMALE"

    By Ethlie Ann Vare

ONE MINUTE MILLIONAIRE"

    By Mark Victor Hanson

    and Robert Allen

"HOW TO WIN FRIENDS AND INFLUENCE PEOPLE"

By Dale Carneige

"RAINMAKER"

By Jeffrey Fox

"THE TIPPING POINT"

By Malcolm Gladwell

STARMAKER MACHINERY

ABOUT THE AUTHOR

Expert talent developer Meredith Day has judged many events such as Casting Director Joey Paul Jensen's prestigious "Best New Talent Awards". Day has developed celebrities such as Jennifer Love Hewitt (Kids Incorporated, Ghost Whisperer, Criminal Minds), Shia LaBeouf (Even Stevens, Transformers), DiDi Benami (American Idol), Jason Castro (American Idol), No Authority (Epic/Sony), Michael Welch (Twilight/Star Trek), Margo Harshman (Even Stevens/NCIS), Adrianne Leon (General Hospital/The Young and the Restless) and Award Nominated young autistic actress/singer Autumn Sky Wolfe (iTunes–AMDA). Meredith Day has guided multiple child and adult performers to great success in the Entertainment Industry, both for the screen and music industry. Her groundbreaking, visionary book "A.D.D. To Excellent Without Drugs" sold out upon release in 1997. Day has not only mentored individual children and adults to success, she has conducted seminars and workshops for talented performers and their managers or parents. Having been a talent developer and talent manager for decades, Day is sharing her expertise with everyone through her groundbreaking books. Day's phenomenal self esteem building "Subliminal Lullaby", sung by award nominated autistic singer Autumn Sky Wolfe and renown star performer and vocal director Debra Byrd, is available on all music download sites.

www.StarmakerMachinery.com

www.ingramcontent.com/pod-product-compliance
Lightning Source LLC
Chambersburg PA
CBHW071617080526
44588CB00010B/1163